THE PRESCRIPTION

The Blueprint for Breaking into Commercial Real Estate and Closing Multi-Million-Dollar Deals

KEN ASHLEY, CCIM, MCR, SIOR

The Prescription:
The Blueprint for Breaking into Commercial
Real Estate and Closing Multi-Million-Dollar Deals

ISBN Paperback: 979-8-89576-177-9
ISBN Hardback: 979-8-89576-178-6

Published by:

"LUCK IS WHAT HAPPENS WHEN PREPARATION MEETS OPPORTUNITY."

—Seneca

Table of Contents

Preface

This project has been a LONG time coming. I've been talking about a book for some years, and finally, the project happened. As I finalize these words for *The Prescription*, I'm struck by the profound truth that success in any arena, be it the high-stakes world of commercial real estate brokerage or the quiet triumphs of a life well-lived, is rarely a solo endeavor.

This book, born from nearly three decades of navigating deals, deadlines, and the unpredictable rhythms of the market, is more than a guide to breaking into tenant representation or closing that elusive lease. It's a testament to the people who've shaped my path, the lessons they've imparted, and the unyielding belief that with the right strategy, mindset, and support, anyone can prescribe their own future in this dynamic industry.

None of this would be possible without the unwavering love and partnership of my wife of 33 years, Karen. She is my biggest fan, confidante, and the steady hand that has grounded me through every market crash and boom. Karen, your encouragement has been the foundation of every page here, reminding me that the best investments are the ones we make in each other.

To my four incredible children—Jonathan and Noah, who are carving their own paths in commercial real estate, carrying forward the grit and ingenuity I've tried to instill; Meghan, whose spirit lights up every room; and Anna, whose wisdom belies her years—thank you for being my greatest joy and motivation. Watching you thrive inspires me daily, proving that the real legacy of this work is the doors it opens for the next generation.

I owe a deep debt of gratitude to the good people at Cushman & Wakefield, whose collaborative spirit and relentless pursuit of excellence have defined my career. A special nod to Mike Elting, who took a chance on me all those years ago and hired me into this extraordinary firm, setting the stage for everything that followed. And to Brad Smith, who first said the words "tenant rep" at a formative and life-changing breakfast, igniting a passion that still burns bright today.

Shout-out as well to Chip Patterson, who gave a wide-eyed newcomer a shot at valeting cars when I was just starting out; your trust in that moment opened doors I didn't even know existed.

To my business partner of 28 years, Sam Hollis, whose sharp insights, shared vision, and unbreakable camaraderie have turned challenges into triumphs. Sam, we've built something special together, and for that, I'm eternally grateful.

To all who have walked this road with me—mentors, colleagues, clients—you know who you are. This book is for you, too: a roadmap drawn from real battlefields, designed to equip aspiring brokers with the tools not just to survive, but to prescribe success in a world where every square foot tells a story.

My brothers, Mike and Walker, are also great friends. I respect each one of you immensely, and I'm proud of your own career successes. Thanks for supporting me in good times and bad.

Finally, to my parents, Roy and Toine. Dad taught me so much. The quiet confidence he had in me keeps me going to this very day. Dad was a master of relationship building, and he was a joy to watch in his element. My Mom, the schoolteacher, kept me on the straight and narrow and was a constant source of guidance, support, and a walking Wikipedia page for every fact you can imagine.

As we stand on the threshold of tomorrow's opportunities, remember the words of Helen Keller: "What we have once enjoyed we can never lose. All that we love deeply becomes a part of us." With that in mind, know this: the future of commercial real estate is not just bright; it's yours to illuminate.

Here's to you, dear reader. I am prescribing bold, brilliant tomorrows for you. And when you get there, I will take great joy in your success.

The Beginning

I've worked as a commercial real estate tenant representative for 30 years, and I wake up unemployed every morning.

And I have carried that knowledge with me every business day for decades.

My boss is me, and the boss has a strong drive to succeed and serve clients. I have a tough boss!

A commercial real estate broker who works as a tenant rep is a specialized broker who helps companies solve their real estate problems. The tenant rep is only compensated when leases are executed. However, that compensation can be very lucrative; the bigger the risk (hopefully), the greater the reward.

Companies sign leases when they need to, not when the tenant rep needs money! Thus, the feeling of unemployment and the resulting "lumpy cash flow."

I have no idea how much money I will earn in any one year as an office tenant representative. But I have the opportunity to make more than many movie stars and CEOs. There is always the possibility of "lumpy cash flow," which can mean earning zero dollars for extended periods of time.

However, as another broker once told me, "It would be boring to know what your compensation will be on January 1! Every year is an adventure." Boy, was he right!

I believe that commercial real estate brokerage (CRE) is the greatest profession in the world. But perhaps I am a little biased, having practiced for over 30 years.

In one form or another, many of those in my family who came before me were involved in, or made a living from, the commercial built environment. My dad was a commercial landscape architect. My grandfather was a general contractor. So was his father. Even so, I needed someone outside of my family to help open the door and explain the business of commercial real estate brokerage to me.

Enter Brad Smith, who at the time worked as a tenant representative of commercial companies. He was kind enough to take me to breakfast and explain at a high level how things work in the somewhat mysterious world of CRE. Brad also gave me the names of some people to call and a rough game plan to follow at the beginning. His advice turned out to be the gift of a lifetime for me.

A big tip of the hat to you, Brad!

Today, decades after that breakfast, I've had many, many breakfasts of my own where I've tried to help young people determine if the business was right for them and, if so, what to do next.

I believe firmly in reaching back down the career ladder, as so many did for me. I'll spend the rest of my life paying back the kind and amazing investment Brad made in me. This book is part of that effort to support those who come after me in this wonderful career.

When I meet with a young person, I often take a blank piece of paper and write their name at the top. In bold letters, I write "Real Estate Prescription." Then I list six to eight tasks for them to complete, such as books/podcasts to consume, and I give them a deadline. Then I sign at the bottom and send them on their way to complete the "prescription."

I've written prescriptions many times and often with good effect. So, if you are reading this, you can now create your own *Real Estate Prescription* and decide whether this career is for you or not.

Being Successful

Let's talk about success at the very top.

You've picked up this book and are considering a career in commercial real estate. You've heard you can make big money (true), but you are wondering what it takes to win at this game. The upside has no cap, but as I said above, the downside is zero.

As I've reflected on my career over the years, I've kept a list of keys to success.

Here are some traits I think are important:

1. **Sales Ability:** Sales is the ability to speak and listen with the intention of convincing someone that you are qualified to assist them. Personality matters, and the ability to get someone to like and trust you is paramount.

2. **Marketing:** Developing a market "brand." In other words, what do people think about you before you walk in the room?

3. **Tactical Listening:** Most people aren't really good listeners. That's why those who have this skill stand out.

4. **Focus:** Focus on the client's problems, not your services. You will be successful not because of what you sell, but because of the problems you solve.

5. **Persistence and Resilience:** Having the discipline to follow and respectfully stay in front of prospects is important. And when you do not get hired, the ability to let the loss roll off your back like a duck sheds water is critical. Also, the ability to fully commit is important. A friend of mine says, "When I commit to something, I will be hugging the deck chairs on the Titanic going down. I am in until the end."

6. **Storytelling and Communications Skills:** Can you tell a story? Do you know how to get people to like you? Can you be succinct

(and tell a less than three-minute story)? We'll discuss all this later in the book.

7. **Networking skills:** Do you know how to work a cocktail party? Hint, it has nothing to do with alcohol!

8. **Tech savvy:** Can you use tools to replace low-payback activities so you can focus on your highest and best use?

9. **Negotiation skills:** Yes, I know you realize this is important, but you must continue to develop negotiation skills until you are a master. Your clients are counting on you.

10. **Market knowledge:** Whatever your market niche is, you can learn it as you get started in the business, but a deep understanding of your market area or vertical will differentiate you. Initially, you need to have intellectual curiosity about your market and a passion to learn it thoroughly.

11. **Long-term focus:** CRE brokerage is a game that takes years to play. Most would say three years minimum to see if you will be successful. I call this a "get-rich-slow" profession.

12. **Hustle:** They say you can't teach hustle, and "they" are right. Either you have the deep-seated desire to hurry down the road of success, or you don't.

13. **Manage Fear:** This is an anxiety-provoking business. I've spent many a night lying in bed, wondering if I would be successful or worrying about a deal. You need a lifeline; someone to speak with or a process to get you through the tough times. After a while, the fear subsides and gives way to self-confidence because you've made it through.

14. **Humility:** When you finally reach the other side and achieve some success, you feel great. It's tempting to strut your stuff, but this is not a good look. Clients and colleagues alike don't want to see you show off. Put your head down and perform, and let others say good things about you.

If you have, or could develop these 14 traits, keep reading.

How to Use This Book

I wanted to create a resource for you that helps you understand commercial real estate brokerage (which can sometimes be pretty opaque) and provides advice and tips on how to get involved (which I imagine is why you picked up this book). Feel free to flip around to the different chapters in this book. Some people will want to read it all the way through, but many will flip to the sections that are most applicable to them.

I hope that we will work together to develop YOUR Real Estate Prescription.

What the Book Is and What It Isn't

What this book is: It is focused on helping individuals decide whether they want to enter a commercial real estate brokerage of almost any kind.

What this book isn't: This book is not a comprehensive overview of ALL the careers in commercial real estate. I touch on them in a high-level way, but if you are interested in a career in real estate investing, asset management, or property management, for example, there may be other sources of information that are more specific to those career paths.

The Prescription is divided into three sections:

Section One: On Understanding describes the industry as a whole and explains the various types of brokers and their methods of earning a living. It also offers a brief description of a few parallel jobs, such as asset management.

Section Two: On Getting Hired provides planning elements to help you transition from watching Netflix on the couch to your first day at your new brokerage.

Section Three: On Succeeding is a roadmap to excellence and success in your career in commercial real estate brokerage.

In between sections, I share a story from my career.

The combination of these three sections is your personal Real Estate Prescription.

Notably, the book is focused on what I have spent my career doing: being a broker. More specifically, my job is to represent tenants/corporate space users in executing their real estate plan. The book will also be a valuable resource if you are interested in representing landlords as well.

Professionally, I have worked as a tenant representative for three decades. That means I represent companies, not buildings. Put another way, my team and I help businesses solve real estate problems.[1]

My clients lease commercial real estate in the Americas and around the world. That is the lens through which I view commercial real estate. If you are considering a career as a real estate investor, developer, asset manager, property manager, or similar profession that doesn't work as a broker, you can gain some information from this book, but just know I think of this from the perspective of a real estate broker as opposed to the owner. Look for a specialty book on entering those other careers, or take a friend who works in that career to lunch and ask them about their experiences.

As you read this book, I hope you will create a plan of action to enter and excel in this business. I've found that individuals who ask the most questions and then listen to the answers are more likely to win.

---

[1] An office tenant representative (tenant rep) is a commercial real estate broker who exclusively represents the interests of tenants seeking office space, guiding them through the leasing process to secure favorable terms without any allegiance to landlords or property owners. Their primary responsibilities include identifying suitable office properties, negotiating lease agreements, analyzing market conditions, and ensuring the tenant's needs for location, size, amenities, and budget are met to minimize costs and risks.

A form to begin to create your personal real estate prescription can be found in *Appendix 1*. Download this prescription to your tablet or print it out to create your personalized approach to getting hired in commercial real estate brokerage.

Why Is It So Difficult to Get Into Commercial Brokerage?

Commercial brokerage is a commission-only profession. You would think it wouldn't be hard to get involved as a service provider in commercial real estate. *They don't have to pay me a salary, so why won't they give me a chance?*

One of the major reasons that commercial real estate brokerages are very selective is that they have "desk costs" that accrue, whether you earn commissions or not. The brokerage provides the physical space for you to conduct your business, along with technology such as real estate databases, computers, and assistance to help with producing materials, insurance, etc. In many states, you're legally required to work under a licensed broker, so the brokerage also enables you to legally practice real estate. Given all the services and amenities the broker provides, even if you were working for free, it isn't free for the brokerage. There is a very real cost to each person on the floor.

Leadership officials in a commercial brokerage are somewhat similar to an investment manager. Instead of picking stocks, the leader is picking people. And the bets can be long-term. Most brokers will tell you that it takes three years to become successful (or not). Let's consider the economic investment your broker has made in you. If desk costs are $350,000 a year, which they could well be at large shops, then the firm is *investing over a million dollars in you.*

Brokerage leadership is also looking for individuals who are smart (of course) but who also fit into the culture of their shop. You can learn much about the culture from the leader, but meeting with the troops can also be very revealing.

At the end of the day, the brokerage leader and the real estate professional enter into what I call the "grand bargain." In this arrangement, the leader is looking for someone who can quickly become self-sufficient, align with the company culture, and ultimately thrive. The leader can make A LOT of money off top-performing brokers. If leadership can "raise their own" top brokers rather than recruiting them from another shop, so much the better.

Now, let's turn to what you and I, the humble broker "producer," are looking for.

The brokerage professional is seeking a "brand" in a shop that will allow them to excel in the marketplace. The saying is that your card helps get you in the door, but the rest is up to you. True. However, the producer also likely needs a comprehensive set of benefits, training, tools, and parallel professionals (an analyst, for example) to maximize success. Of course, the producer is also looking for aggressive sharing in the revenue they generate. This concept is called "sharing splits," but as we will discuss in Part 2, "splits" are only one component of the brokerage partnership evaluation.

The payoff to the brokerage company is also predicated upon your staying in place. Finding the right culture and mentorship for you is as important to the broker as it is to the brokerage. When it works, amazing things can happen, and I've seen it time and time again. People from all walks of life can earn a very handsome living. The broker (company) wins, and clients get excellent service. A trifecta.

This book is dedicated to helping you find your own grand bargain.

300 Months

After talking to 13 different commercial real estate firms over a series of months, I'd gotten an offer from the only one I REALLY wanted to join: Cushman & Wakefield. I was elated and bursting with pride.

Karen and I had dinner in our very small house in a suburb of Atlanta. She didn't know my news, but I was positively giddy, so she knew something was up.

Over spaghetti and meatballs, I told her all about it. In great detail. Cushman & Wakefield was going to be our big break. I was going to slay dragons, and we were going to make it big.

There was one issue, though: I was to work 100% at risk in a commission-only environment. There was no limit to my upside, but my earnings downside was...zero.

Even though they offered, I never wanted a "draw" (a loan, essentially), and I was prepared for the risk. We had no kids, and Karen had a good job at EY. In those days, there was no real training program at C&W, but I had a degree in sales and sales management. However, any way you sliced it, the risk was extraordinary.

Suddenly, as I was slurping noodles, Karen held up her hands. After 30 minutes of me talking, she had heard enough and she had something to say. I thought she was going to talk about the social plans for the weekend.

Her mouth was tight, but her eyes sparkled, and she looked right into my eyes. She finally spit it out, "I'm pregnant!" I was happy and terrified in the same moment. "Uh, that's great!" I said with true enthusiasm, but I felt a pang in the pit of my stomach.

I knew I had nine months to make it. Or not. In the business of commercial real estate.

The In Between

After the Great Revelation of Karen's pregnancy, I called a number of friends to ask for help with side jobs. I started valeting cars the very next weekend, working till 2:00 a.m. on Friday and 4:00 a.m. on Saturday. I managed property on the side for a few owners. I joined the local fire department and, after training, worked part-time shifts for pay. I would do basically anything legal to build our cash reserves. Babies are expensive, after all.

Meanwhile, at work, things weren't going so well. I was cold calling my brains out in a gritty industrial area of Atlanta, but I couldn't hit a lick. I had been selling things since I was in second grade, and I was good at it. But it is immensely hard to talk to a decision-maker and build trust when you are so young and still learning about your chosen field. I can clearly remember the dual fear of not making any meetings, as well as the concern of what to say if a decision-maker picked up the phone.

I've never been so depressed in my life. The rejection was omnipresent, and I couldn't sleep at night. Every morning, I stared at myself in the mirror and wondered what the hell I'd gotten myself into. And I thought about my wife and unborn baby and the requirement that I perform to take care of them. The responsibility and pressure to succeed were overwhelming.

I Quit

After eight and a half months without a penny of income, I had had enough. I was going to quit.

It was Friday, and I marched into my manager Mike Elting's office. I told him all my troubles and he listened carefully. At the end of my speech, he took off his glasses and paused. He looked directly at me and quietly said, "Bring me your deal sheet."

I ran to my cube and grabbed the document. I handed it to him, panting. Mike looked at it and finally looked up at me. "Hmmmm," he said, "you have some potential here."

Then he asked me a strange question. "Ken, do you know what sunk cost is?" I stammered, "Sure, we studied that in Econ, but what does that have to do with this situation?"

"You've spent nearly nine months of your life here making no income. How long would it take you to make this back in a regular salary job, and what would your salary be?"

I took a guess and we did the math together. It would take four-and-a-half years to make back the past eight-and-a-half months of "at risk" comp IF I could get other employment immediately.

Mike gently said, "Why don't you stay around a little longer and see if you can be successful?"

Surprise!

I thought about my conversation with Mike for a long time. I sat in my car in the garage, debating the issue in my head. I didn't realize it at the time, but this was literally a life-changing decision either way. Finally, I cranked up my car and headed home.

The next morning, after a very restless night of sleep, I had made a decision. I took Mike's advice for two reasons. One, his confidence in me meant everything. I can't tell you how important a few words of support from a senior person are in a young broker's life. Mike is a great listener and a leader who just makes you feel good when you are around him.

Second, I played out a conversation in my head. I'd have to tell my father that I had quit and that I was a failure. I simply couldn't bring myself to do so, no matter the risk to my income. My dad's opinion of me was paramount. I would park even more cars and find more jobs. That morning, I looked at myself in the mirror with a new resolve. I AM GOING TO MAKE IT, I said out loud. I hit the road to the office with a new resolve and a commitment like I've never felt before in my life.

About two weeks later, I got a call I hadn't been expecting: a deal was moving ahead! I felt like parading around the office, and I wanted to cheer as if the Georgia Bulldogs had scored a touchdown. Instead, I shouted under my breath and pumped my fist in the air. The day the deal was made is still one of the better days of my life.

Karen was elated, too. She wanted her man to make it, and I could see the relief in her eyes as I experienced my very first success in commercial real estate. I had my confidence back!

Karen and I talked about the money from the surprise deal. We had many needs, but one was more important than all others. I took some of the commission dollars from my first deal and went to an estate sale the following weekend.

We used the money to buy the four-poster bed we sleep in to this very day. Real estate at first caused me to sleep poorly, but in the wink of an eye, I was sleeping like a baby!

300 Months Later

Well, I've been at Cushman & Wakefield for 25 years this month: 300 months! Our dreams DID come true; I've been blessed with great clients and teammates. We've done OK, Karen and I. We ended up having four great kids and still love each other very much. Our oldest son, Jonathan, recently got engaged to be married, which, of course, we are thrilled about. Yes, the same child that Karen mentioned in our "real estate spaghetti" dinner.

And I still feel that desire to keep succeeding, but it's much more about winning to support my team and those around me. The bottom line is I wake up unemployed every morning, and it's up to me to do the right things on the path to winning and executing for our clients.

In the evening, as I make my way to bed and look at the beautiful four-poster bed we bought with my first commission dollars, I think about the impact we all can have on others in ways we may not realize. Mike Elting will always be a hero to me. His clutch advice and quiet confidence in me saved my real estate career. But many others helped me along the way, and for that I am so grateful.

Now it is my turn to help others. I frequently take calls with young people who are trying to get started or are new in the business. Reaching back down the ladder is a sacred obligation.

To clear the record, the modern-day training and support at Cushman & Wakefield is industry-leading. I take great pride in my company's top position in our industry regarding the careers of young people. I know our young brokers know exactly what to say when the decision-maker takes their call.

Oh, and one more thing. Marrying well is so critical for life success. I love my wife with all my heart, and her support, thousands of times in our marriage, has made all the difference. Growing old(er) together has been one of the greatest things to happen to me.

It's been a great run, and I look forward to many more years of real estate, gray hair, and all. And I now fully understand, in Technicolor, the concept of sunk costs; thanks, Mike!

But I also now know the formula for calculated risk: hard work + a strong dose of mentorship. That equals 25 wonderful years at C&W, an amazing family, and a pretty terrific bed.

SECTION ONE

On Understanding Commercial Real Estate

CHAPTER 1

Introduction to Commercial Real Estate

"Do not let what you cannot do interfere with what you can do." —John Wooden

I'm excited that you're excited about commercial real estate. If you choose to work as a service provider (broker) in this industry, you can achieve an extremely high income. Of course, another result is that you may achieve no income or very little income. Where there is great risk, there should be great reward.

I'm going to take a few moments to go macro to micro to explain the industry.

Residential Vs Commercial: An Imperfect Comparison

I want to start by defining the distinction between commercial and residential real estate.

When people think about commercial real estate, most see it through the lens of residential real estate, which is an imperfect comparison.

In residential real estate, the purpose is to accommodate someone's need for a home. The entire deal centers on finding a place to live and is therefore not a commercial real estate transaction. Most importantly, there's no cash flow to an investor; rather, there's money invested at the beginning of the hold period and then money out when the home is sold.

Emotions are a big deal in residential real estate. For instance, a couple can have issues before they even start looking for houses, and those issues can manifest during the deal and make life complicated.

Conversely, the commercial real estate industry is built first on a business proposition. If you are a company that needs real estate, you plan to use it as a tool to conduct business.

If you are a commercial real estate investor, you can expect a periodic cash flow, regardless of the property type. Most typically, there will be a monthly cash flow, also known as rent. At the end of your investment period, you will sell the asset, also known by its technical name, the "reversion."

To sum up the differences: residential ownership isn't usually about business. It is about finding a place to lay your head. The brokers who support home buyers need to be available when their clients are, which means nights and weekends. Commercial brokerage is about helping businesses solve their problems with effective real estate decisions. Commercial brokers do dinners, but not much happens over the weekend. Well, once you are successful, anyway!

To help you begin to understand the commercial real estate industry, I categorize it into two simple categories: Owners and Corporate Users.

The Commercial Real Estate T-Bar

Ownership	Corporation
Building Ownership/ Ultimate Owner ↓ Asset Manager ↓ Property Manager ↓ Leasing Broker	Corporate Tenant ↓ Board of Directors ↓ Top Executive Resp. for Commercial Real Estate (i.e., CFO) ↓ Real Estate Director ↙ ↘ Tenant Representative Project Manager

This T-bar helps us simplify the industry and provides a straightforward way to understand the motivations of different players.

*Top Executive Responsible for Commercial Real Estate

Ownership

As you can see in the diagram, on the left-hand side, we have the ownership piece. Ownership can take various forms, ranging from a family office or a high-net-worth individual owning the entire asset. More likely, though, there is a partnership or some other form of entity that owns the building.

When there are multiple owners (and sometimes when a single owner controls), there is usually an asset manager. This individual's job is to effectively serve as the "mayor" of the asset. They make final decisions on annual budgets, leasing transactions, and expenditures for repairs and maintenance. The asset manager is held accountable for metrics that can include the Internal Rate of Return, Debt Service Coverage Ratio, or Unlevered Cash Flow, for example.

Below the asset manager is a property manager who can employ folks who perform building maintenance and cleaning. They may contract out some services, such as janitorial, and simply supervise. The property manager is also responsible for ensuring that tenants are happy and that their day-to-day needs are met.

Finally, we arrive at the property leasing team, also known as the landlord brokers. They field calls from tenant reps with prospects for the building and try to get the building added to the tour list. They attend industry events and know the most productive tenant reps very well. Landlord brokers show space as well, of course! They play a very important role, as their personality can "brighten" up a building. If the agents are charismatic, good conversationalists, and can "storytell" about the asset, then owners know they stand a better chance of making a short list. We all love to see a good salesperson at work! Landlord brokers also generate proposals to lease prospects and lead the negotiations when they are underway. Being a landlord broker is a big job and can be highly rewarding. Making large transactions can be lucrative, and it's fun to drive by "your" asset and tell your family about all the deals you made there.

Corporate Users

The right-hand side of our T-bar represents the consumer or the user of the real estate. The user is frequently referred to as the tenant or, in some cases, the occupier of the real estate asset. One of the big differences between the owner and the tenant is that the owner is a professional real estate investor trying to earn a return on their capital. The tenant is in another business but uses real estate as a way to advance their business.

In a post-COVID world, we can debate whether you need to go to the office, but offices still exist. Industrial users continue to need warehouses, regardless of the circumstances. You can't work from home in the warehouse business!

Back to the T-bar. On the right-hand side, we show the board of directors as the ultimate authority, although shareholders are where the buck stops. Unless the entity is closely held, the board makes the final call.

Below the board is the highest-ranking executive responsible for real estate. This role is often filled by the chief financial officer (CFO), but it may also be held by a chief administrative officer (CAO) or a chief operating officer (COO).

Next is the role of real estate director. Real estate director is not a job in every company. Small companies with, say, less than $100 million in sales may have another executive, like the CFO, handle real estate off the "side of their desk." Either the smaller company cannot afford a salary for a real estate director, or their portfolio is relatively small and can be managed by a part-time professional.

Finally, we come to the tenant representative. I've covered their role in detail in Chapter 3, but in short, a tenant rep is responsible for identifying property options, preparing and presenting a survey, conducting tours, negotiating business terms, and coordinating with attorneys to finalize the lease.

Different Types of Commercial Real Estate

This T-Bar paradigm applies to what I call "the different flavors of ice cream," which include office, industrial, retail, medical office, buildings, and even data centers.

Of course, different asset classes have different specializations. Data center brokers are very different from medical office brokers in what they need to know.

You might wonder how someone learns to become competent in a particular specialty. It's through what I call the "blacksmith method." They typically work for a senior broker for several years to learn the ropes. They also attend industry conferences of their type of real estate and learn from executives running the companies in their niche.

My niche in commercial real estate is a focus on "multi-market accounts." I represent a number of clients (some publicly traded) that have portfolios of leased space. These various locations can be offices or industrial facilities. My team and I help our clients manage "critical dates," which include lease expiration dates and option notice dates. This means we inform them when to initiate a transaction to either renew, move, close, or open a new location, all at the client's direction. We lead the search process and business terms negotiation and, in conjunction with legal counsel, advise on the lease document.

The bottom line is that if you can make money from leasing or selling an asset, it can be classified as commercial real estate.

CHAPTER 2

The Commercial Real Estate Industry

"Business, like life, is all about how you make people feel. It's that simple, and it's that hard."
—Danny Meyer

To delve deeper into the industry, I thought I'd take a moment to describe Commercial Real Estate (CRE). Have you ever seen a large building with many people coming and going? Of course you have! That's commercial real estate. It's where businesses operate, and people shop and live. It is where we operate much of our lives. Did you go out for dinner last night? Did you watch a movie? Maybe you drove there in your new car? Did you wear that new outfit from an online seller? All are supported by commercial real estate. Retail delivered the final experience, but the food and clothes came from a warehouse, supported by executives who sit in an office.

Commercial real estate impacts everything.

Commercial real estate is important to both people and the economy because it provides places for businesses to operate and supports local governments through property taxes. It also helps to create jobs and stimulate economic growth. How many times have you seen pictures of joyous public officials cutting the ribbon on a new facility that will generate many new jobs? Commercial real estate is a big economic deal. In 2023, the commercial real estate industry contributed $2.5 trillion to the U.S. Gross Domestic Product.[2] That's a lot of money! The industry also supported more than 15 million jobs. Commercial real estate is the engine of our economy. Let's put the pedal to the metal!

There are many different types of commercial real estate, including office buildings, retail stores, warehouses, and hotels.

Not to oversimplify, but just to be clear: Office buildings are where businesses have their offices. Retail stores are where people buy goods and services. Warehouses are where goods are stored. Hotels are where people stay when they are traveling.

In each major category, there are classes and subcategories. "Class" refers to the asset's age, location, and condition. The class methodology is a shorthand term used by investors, owners, and brokers to convey the condition and age of an asset.

For example, a **Class A** top-quality office building is usually located at Main and Main, of relatively new construction, includes or is near top amenities, and has excellent credit tenants.

Class B assets are the goldilocks of commercial real estate. Not too hot and not too cold. They are aging; however, tenants can find some real bargains in terms of leasing rates compared to the new, high-end Class A buildings. The key in Class B is strong due diligence to ensure the landlord is financially sound and that major items such as roof, structure, HVAC, elevator, and other major systems are up to date.

In contrast, a **Class C** office building is located in a rough neighborhood, is old and considered outdated, and may have an eclectic collection of tenants. Frequently, Class C offerings may be on the edge of compliance with building codes and may be "grandfathered" in on evolutions of

---

[2] NAIOP Research Foundation. Economic Impacts of Commercial Real Estate 2024.

building best practices. There are still buildings today in New York, Chicago, and beyond that, which do NOT have sprinklers. They were built before the thinking on fire suppression changed, and installing sprinklers is usually too cost-prohibitive.

Subcategories

Subcategories involve specialties within the category. While delving into each subcategory is beyond the scope of this book, let's take a look at industrial real estate as one example to give you an idea of what I'm talking about.

Industrial Real Estate

A Class A facility is likely new, features a really high ceiling height, and is very large. Many facilities are well over a million square feet. Class B industrial is very different. Although they may have some age, Class B products feature small suites (called bays) that support landscapers, plumbers, electricians, and similar professionals. Class C is likely in a poor location and may have less expensive elements, such as metal siding.

There are also many special-purpose types of real estate. Examples include self-storage facilities, cell phone antennas, farmland, ports, churches, graveyards, and many other types of properties.

Investing

In addition to viewing real estate through the lens of business use, investing offers a distinct perspective on these assets. Commercial real estate can be a very good investment. It can provide a steady income stream and can appreciate in value over time.

The tax benefits can also be epic, because the government uses the tax code to incentivize investors to create more commercial real estate. We need more housing, warehouses, medical office buildings, office buildings, and other commercial spaces. Uncle Sam can waive his magic wand and make the investment attractive so that capital flows towards "sticks and bricks."

However, it is important to do your research before investing in commercial real estate. Several factors must be considered, including location, property type, and current market conditions.

If you are interested in learning more about commercial real estate, there are several resources available to you. You can talk to a real estate agent or broker, or you can read books and articles about the industry. Commercial real estate can be a great way to invest your money and build wealth. It is a big and important industry that provides jobs and economic growth.

What's Next?

Now that you understand the basic categories of real estate, you can start asking experts about the pros and cons of working in each segment. Some areas, like retail, tend to have high transaction volume but relatively low fees per deal. Others, such as specialties like office headquarters or large industrial properties, may offer much higher commissions but involve fewer transactions overall.

Much of the decision of which industry to pursue is based, of course, on your interests, but also on your risk tolerance. If someone is doing many transactions, do they have a greater opportunity to make a living? If they're only conducting a few transactions a year, the risk is much higher, especially if a transaction falls apart. Some will pick a commercial real estate niche based on their degree. If you are an engineer, perhaps industrial is for you. If you have a science background, medical could make sense. Talking with brokers with expertise may help you make your decision. We discuss later in the book how to get a meeting with brokers. Just know that a good "advice meeting" can go a long way. Be sure to ask them for comments on both the good *and* the bad of their vertical.

Finally, I want to put your mind at ease about something. Just because you start in one vertical does not mean you have to stay there for your entire career. For example, I started my career as an industrial broker. Now, I am designated as an office broker. I work in industrial as well, which is a good thing!

You can change. Just make the best, most informed decision you can with the information you have now, and get after it!

CHAPTER 3

What Does a Broker Do? A Day in the Life

"The greatest glory in living lies not in never falling,
but in rising every time we fall." —Nelson Mandela

A commercial real estate broker is compensated for only a few things. 1) Developing and maintaining relationships that lead to profitable business, 2) supporting businesses in their real estate needs (or ownership if you are a landlord broker), and 3) getting transactions closed (which by implication means you understand, support, and deliver for your client).

Everything else supports these three imperatives. Market knowledge, check. Understanding the construction and operations of a building, sure. Knowing how to read and provide comments on a lease to make it marketable, absolutely.

More generally, you have to be a self-starter. I often say, "You can't teach hustle." When no one else is looking, will you do the hard things and the "right" things to propel your practice forward? If you need someone with a whistle and a bullhorn watching your every move, commercial brokerage isn't for you.

Self-confidence will develop over time, but you need to have the courage to pick up the phone, make the pitch, and deliver value when working with your team. Commercial real estate brokerage is akin to consulting; you must deliver results.

Another issue to contemplate is dealing with rejection. Different people handle this differently. I will tell you, I do feel the pain of a big loss (say, on a pitch to get hired), but I know myself. It takes me about 24 hours to process the loss, then I smile and move on. As my first senior broker used to say, "Every 'No' gets you closer to the next 'Yes'!"

How to Choose Where to Start Your Career

The first thing I want you to know is that choosing one way into commercial real estate does <u>not</u> mean you have eliminated other CRE career options. I've seen many people start in research and move to brokerage, or start in brokerage but move to a salary-plus-bonus gig like working for an "end user" and helping a company run its real estate portfolio.

The analogy I frequently use with young people is that of a circus tent. Commercial real estate is one big circus, and you just need to get under the tent. You may start with feeding the livestock, even though you want to be an acrobat. However, once you get into the tent, you'll be part of the show, and you will meet people. Networking is a lot easier when you are IN an industry!

Back to your career. The biggest initial driver of which career you choose to pursue in commercial real estate has to do with your risk tolerance. If you are interested in the industry but want a regular paycheck, there are options available to you on both sides of the equation. If you are an individual who can tolerate higher risk, then being a broker could be an opportunity for you.

Also, I would point out that you can likely tolerate more risk at the beginning of your career. If you are unmarried or not in a committed relationship, then you may not have children to support. Once others begin to depend on you for support, your risk of failure becomes greater.

At the beginning of a career, most folks find themselves in an "asset light" position, meaning they may not own a home and hopefully don't have huge debt beyond student loans. Therefore, the monthly living costs for someone in their early years are likely much lower than those of a mid-career professional with the proverbial mortgage, school tuition, and country club dues.

To determine whether you would prefer to represent a landlord or a tenant in your area, I recommend meeting with professionals in both fields. Ask questions and get a firsthand understanding of what a typical day in the life of their careers would be like.

I call these initial exploratory meetings "advice meetings." We will discuss scheduling meetings in more detail later in the book, but it's essential to be respectful of anyone who gives you their time. Do pay attention to the basics, including researching that individual in advance, asking really good questions you've prepared, and following up with a *thank-you* note immediately after the meeting.

Tenant Rep Brokers

In this section, I will outline the key responsibilities of successful tenant representatives. Hint: money or commission income is an outcome of success in service, not the other way around.

Essentially, a tenant rep broker is an expert who helps business executives find solutions to their real estate problems. They not only have an understanding of the "sticks and bricks," but also how the business operates and why it needs real estate. Executives will assume you're a market expert, but you can differentiate yourself by helping their business understand its market fit. For example, taking too much or too little space is a constant source of concern with corporate executives. Partnering with experts, such as architects who can help forecast demand, can add real value to the tenant rep's portfolio of services.

Also, the best tenant reps can bring a level of business wisdom to a problem. They are pleasant to be around and are exceptional listeners. Always professional, the broker takes the time to take notes and can recall conversations they had months ago.

The very best tenant reps can politely tell a client "no" if they think a project is headed in the wrong direction. The tenant rep partners with the client to support the business imperative rather than just the real estate solution. I often tell clients that commercial real estate is how I help business leaders solve problems. The building is not the means to an end, but only part of helping them with their problem.

So, let's get back to what a tenant rep actually does. In a nutshell, the tenant rep is responsible for three things: finding and securing new business, working deals as they come along, and nurturing client relationships.

Most of my career has been spent helping clients lease space, so that is the lens through which I write the next few paragraphs. Brokers can utilize a variety of databases, market knowledge, plus calls to landlords and owners in the community to complete a "property survey." The property survey provides the basic building information, such as address, size, rate, and special features, along with a picture of the subject building.

1. **Real Estate Mandate:** Once the broker fully understands the client's business challenge, they create what I call the "real estate mandate." This document clearly outlines the client's needs and objectives. After the business leader reviews and approves the mandate, the tenant rep begins researching potential space options and takes the deal to market.

2. **Make a list of potential properties:** Once the property survey is of presentation quality, the tenant rep will have a call with the client to select a few options that make sense for them. Many

times, I've seen clients review property surveys and provide new information. For example, they may want a more "walkable" area, more amenities, or to locate in a different "commute shed." It's difficult to know everything about a real estate problem in the first conversation. However, as you present options, additional considerations that shape the business mandate will surface.

3. **Arrange tours of shortlisted properties:** Once you have a shortlist, the tenant rep will arrange tours of the options. The tour is part of what I call an "education process," and I've seen it hundreds of times. Seeing buildings on a piece of paper or a computer screen is only the start. There is nothing like touring a space in person to help you visualize how it will all work together. While it's tempting to think that online touring options can replace a physical tour, I strongly discourage this as the primary decision-making path. Executives will make significant decisions that commit large sums for many years. Taking the time to go on a physical tour is very important.

4. **Request For Proposal (RFP):** After the property tour, the team will reconvene to select a handful of buildings to send a request for proposal (RFP). The RFP allows the tenant representative to ask the landlord specific questions and have them put their answers in writing.

5. **Side-By-Side Analysis:** Once all the RFPs are gathered, the tenant rep or an analyst team member will create a side-by-side analysis of all the properties. This side-by-side, called an "executive dashboard," helps the business team understand the particulars of each property compared to the others, including financial costs.

6. **Counteroffers:** Upon review of the executive dashboard, the client will select three or four options to counteroffer. After some back-and-forth negotiations, the tenant representative will guide the client to select a building to proceed to the next step.

7. **Finalizing the Business Terms:** An outcome of the "handshake" can be a letter of intent (LOI), but I often summarize final terms in an email rather than spending a significant amount of time on an interim document. In the United States, LOI's are non-binding, and arguably, we should move to the lease.

8. **Lease Document:** Next, the landlord's attorney will draft the lease document, which must be carefully reviewed by everyone on the tenant side, including the tenant rep. While tenant reps are not allowed to practice law, they certainly can and should read the lease document and weigh in on several fronts. First, they can ensure that the business deal is accurately reflected in the lease. It's amazing how many times I've seen rent tables listed incorrectly in the lease! Undetected inaccuracies can result in errors of hundreds of thousands, or even millions, of dollars in a transaction. In law, there is a doctrine called the "four corners" of the document. In some cases, even if a lease is fully signed and the rent table contains incorrect mathematical calculations, the tenant may still owe the landlord more rent than agreed upon. Also, tenant representatives understand what is and what isn't marketable in terms of legal concepts within the document. They can work with legal counsel to make sure that the document is as favorable to the tenant as possible.

Once the lease has been executed, the end user has space committed for their business needs and can begin the process of fitting out (aka building out the office to their specific needs). I love seeing happy executives when we showcase the new office, warehouse, or other dedicated facility. When the lease is executed by all parties, the tenant rep earns a brokerage fee. As a tenant rep, you may have spent months or even years getting to this point, so it's okay to take a Friday afternoon off and do something fun.

You've got to celebrate success!

Even though the lease has been signed, your work is not yet complete. Good tenant reps stay involved and ensure the client achieves a good result in the build-out of their new space. While tenant reps are not project managers, paying attention on a high level is a good example of service after the sale.

Tenant Rep Models

There are numerous specialties and models within the tenant representation business. I've seen many smart people specialize and do *very* well. Some make more than movie stars. After all, focus, just like a magnifying glass, gives you extreme economic power in the marketplace. A friend of mine likes to say, "The riches are in the niches."

I'd now like to explain some of the basic models for the tenant rep business.

Farmer/Local Market Expert

This is what most people envision a commercial agent doing all day. A local market expert is someone who is a true market expert in a city or even a submarket. One of my colleagues at my shop knows the Atlanta Northwest industrial market cold. It's remarkable to drive around with him because he knows who owns every building, the names of the tenants, and often when their leases expire. He knows market rates and the latest deals. My friend is a walking Wikipedia on that market, and he is a joy to work with.

This specialization is a surefire way to make it as a tenant rep broker. Prospects will immediately see that you know your stuff, which makes it much easier to build trust. Despite the abundance of available data and databases, someone who knows their stuff cold *and* has the wisdom to advise others on what to do next has immense value.

Product Specialist

Pick a "flavor of ice cream." There are many specialties to choose from. Class A industrial, Class B industrial, data center, call center, retail, office, and land are all specialties. While some tenant rep brokers in smaller towns are generalists, most in big cities specialize in a product type and learn as much as they can. They are experts in their niche and can often cite market statistics and recent deals.

These brokers also know a lot about their clients' most common problems and how real estate can solve them. For example, I work as an office tenant rep. I know (as I write this) that returning to the office, the financial safety of landlords, and leasing the right amount of office space are hugely on the minds of my prospects and clients. I write and speak about these issues all the time.

At large real estate shops in major metropolitan areas, you will likely specialize in a specific product type. You certainly can transition. At the beginning of my career, I worked as an industrial broker for two years. Then a senior office guy recruited me to join his team. Now, I'm an office broker.

How to choose? Some choices may be made for you based on which teams in the shop have openings. Of course, if you are passionate about a particular product type, you can seek out the senior brokers who have that specialization and pitch them on your value.

Account Specialist

When I joined my firm, I never even thought of an account model as a way to make a living. Now, it accounts for a significant portion of my annual production. "Accounts" are companies that have portfolios of leased real estate. For example, let's say we secure an exclusive relationship with XYZ Co., a mid-cap company headquartered in

Chicago with 140 offices across North America for knowledge workers and salespeople. Let's say annual revenues are $600 million. Those 140 locations, plus the headquarters, need attention. There are always leases expiring. There are always cases of senior management wanting to close or open an office. There are many times when XYZ Co. buys another company, and locations must be consolidated.

An account specialist does the following:

- Meet with the executive in charge of real estate and understand the company's strategy, including its objectives (e.g., growth, cost reduction, or downsizing).

- Develop one "source of truth" for all those leases. In some cases, companies operate some pretty large portfolios using Excel spreadsheets. My team will "abstract" or summarize the leases and put all the "critical dates," such as expiration dates, in a database. We can manage the portfolio more effectively by consolidating all data in one place, enabling us to quickly find answers to any lease-related questions.

- Run deals. We use some great technology to keep everyone updated, but with a large portfolio, there is always something going on. Many account specialists hold calls as often as weekly to discuss active deals.

- Manage "field brokers." We select local market experts and provide them with our playbook on how to run a deal. We rely on their local expertise to guide us in building selection and in the deal negotiation.

- Generate RFP's (Requests for Proposals). There is certainly an art to asking the landlord the right questions. We invest considerable time in customizing these RFPs to provide the client with the most critical data for their decision-making process.

- Side-by-side dashboards. Once landlords send us proposals, we create side-by-side reports so executives can view the financial summary and key deal terms next to each other.
- Downselect and finalize deal terms with the chosen landlord.
- Read the lease. I teach a whole class on this subject. We can't practice law, but we can help the legal team understand what is considered "market" in terms of lease provisions, AND we verify that the business deal is accurately reflected in the lease draft.
- QBR (Quarterly Business Reviews) (or whatever frequency the client would like). We provide a summary of deals done and progress towards goals, and call out big wins on the client's behalf.

See Chapter 4 for a full discussion on broker compensation. However, to focus specifically on account specialists' compensation for a moment, here is what you need to know: account specialists make a smaller percentage on each deal because they employ field brokers. Field or local brokers receive the deal, typically with little to no pitch or sales effort. Their role is to serve as the market expert, likely overseeing the building tours and the RFP process. In return, field brokers may earn between 25% and 50% of the fee. Field brokers are critical to getting the deal done, and on my team, we work hard to take care of them.

Since they need to be compensated, the field broker's share reduces the fee coming to the account specialist. The good news is that the account team has a pretty good idea that they will be doing multiple deals with XYZ Co, which "de-risks" the brokerage profession, just a little.

Some brokers have a blend of these models. Some are generalists. There is really no wrong way to be a broker as long as you are serving your clients well, protecting and developing your team, and making money!

History Lesson

Another way to understand the tenant rep profession is to have some historical context. After World War II, as businesses expanded significantly in the 1950s and 1960s, many medium- and large-sized businesses employed internal real estate teams.

They were responsible not only for finding but also for operating the business's facilities. I've heard stories about these executives literally walking up and down the streets of New York City, knocking on doors, and meeting with landlords to determine if they had any available space. If that sounds inefficient, I agree with you.

Another significant issue with having internal staff manage real estate is that corporate employees cannot be experts on multiple markets simultaneously. Even if you have a significant understanding of multiple markets, those markets will change over time.

Finally, I tell corporate executives today that they are likely to have one deal at a time in any major American city. I might have multiple. In general, local brokers will work harder and smarter for me because I can send them a lot of business.

In the early 1970s, a few pioneering real estate brokers approached companies to see if they could represent them as tenant representatives, but the tenant rep didn't really exist as a profession—most brokers primarily represented landlords. The idea that a company could have a real estate advisor who worked solely in their best interests was still new.

The tenant rep profession began to mature in the 1980s and 1990s. Today, it's an invaluable part of business. Companies were able to significantly downsize their in-house real estate teams and rely on brokers for the vast majority of corporate real estate transactions in the United States.

Not only did companies benefit from the tenant reps' expertise, but they also no longer had to pay them a fee directly. Those early pioneers established a compensation structure in which landlords pay tenant representatives for their services. The commission is based on a market standard that varies in almost every city and town in America. The corporation ultimately pays the fee when it pays rent, but it doesn't have to write a check through accounts payable, which makes CFOs very happy.

The growth of specialty services, such as tenant reps, led to a behemoth industry that serves companies and investors alike worldwide. Today's large commercial real estate services firms are complex consultancies with extensive resources and a broad geographic spread. To give some context, in 2025, the commercial industry is projected to generate $1.5 trillion in fees.[3]

Other Types of Brokers: Landlord and Capital Markets

Landlord brokers serve an essential function in commercial real estate. Their job is to represent property owners by marketing available spaces and attracting high-quality tenants. One experienced landlord broker once described her job as "differentiating my listing in a sea of sameness." She explained, "My goal is to give a building energy; to tell a story about how this space can be a perfect fit for the tenant. People buy with emotion and justify with facts."

Imagine you're the CEO of a growing company, looking to move your headquarters. You've hired a top tenant rep to find the ideal space. When you visit a potential building, the first person you meet in the lobby might be the landlord broker. That broker's presence, enthusiasm, and

---

[3] IBIS World Market Research. Market size and recent performance (2015-2030). https://www.ibisworld.com/united-states/industry/commercial-real-estate/2009/

professionalism can significantly shape your impression of the space, and even influence your final decision.

A landlord broker does more than just know the property; they bring it to life. They communicate their strengths, address concerns, and frame the space in a way that resonates with prospective tenants. Their ability to present a property with energy, insight, and relevance can make a huge difference in how that property is perceived.

However, the role requires more than just strong presentation skills. Landlord brokers must deeply understand the competitive landscape: what nearby buildings offer, where their property stands out, and what's shifting in the market. Differentiation is key.

Equally important are the relationships they build with tenant reps. These connections help draw attention to listings and build trust in negotiations. At the same time, landlord brokers must maintain strong credibility with the property owner. Whether they work directly for the owner or through a third-party firm, they're expected to protect the building's interests, convey a strong vision for its future, and ensure it's being managed professionally and effectively.

Landlord brokerage encompasses two primary employment models: direct hire by property owners, often seen in publicly traded real estate firms, and third-party engagements via commercial real estate services. While the former typically offers a base salary supplemented by bonuses, the latter is usually commission-based, presenting a higher risk-reward scenario.

This dichotomy between in-house and third-party brokerage illuminates a broader principle within real estate: the balance between guaranteed income and the potential for higher earnings through commission-based roles. Moreover, landlord brokers differ from tenant representatives in their product offering. While the former sells tangible assets, such as "sticks and bricks," the latter provides a service-oriented approach to space acquisition.

The most successful landlord brokers excel in negotiation and economic analysis of transactions and possess a nuanced understanding of construction costs. They not only zealously advocate for their clients but also bring a wealth of knowledge and strategic insight to the table, making them invaluable partners in real estate transactions.

In summary, a career as a landlord broker offers big rewards, from financial compensation to the satisfaction of contributing to important business decisions. However, it also comes with challenges, including the pressure of commission-based income and the demand for constant availability. Despite these difficulties, the landlord broker remains a vital part of the commercial real estate industry, offering meaningful opportunities for those prepared to take on the work.

Capital Markets Brokers

While tenant representatives and landlord brokers help companies lease space, capital markets brokers are in the business of selling real estate, typically assets that generate income for investors. Many large commercial real estate assets, such as office buildings or Class A warehouses, are owned by institutional investors. Those investors deploy capital into real estate and will also occasionally sell assets to complete an investment.

In some cycles, capital markets brokers can be the most highly compensated type of broker. However, this type of brokerage is arguably one of the most complex. Brokers in this segment often initiate a business development process by conducting a formal Broker's Opinion of Value for an asset's owner.

Those opinions will include very complex financial analyses that establish the probabilities of tenants renewing or leaving the asset. If tenants leave the asset, the broker makes additional assumptions about how long it will take to re-lease the vacancy and how much of an investment in improvements and commissions will be required.

A Broker's Opinion of Value also has a market basis of comparison in that it will look at the sales price of other similarly situated assets for comparison purposes. Finally, capital markets brokers are expected to be able to compare assets based on estimated replacement or construction costs.

Once a capital markets broker has been retained by an owner, they will conduct a thorough, detailed evaluation of the asset, including a comprehensive review of all leases and other relevant documents. They will then put together a marketing package for the asset.

Capital markets brokers have great relationships with buyers and sellers of real estate. Their databases are honed over many years and are worth their weight in gold. The brokers will send a teaser of the marketing package to their database and call probable buyers. Interested buyers will fill out a non-disclosure agreement and then gain access to the full package or data room.

Next, the capital markets broker will conduct tours of the asset and hold calls with individuals who have a genuine interest in making a purchase. Then, they will have a call for offers.

Once the offers have been received and a side-by-side comparison prepared, the broker will sit down with their client. At this point, the broker continues to be very valuable to the process because, as important as price is to a seller, so is the ability to close. Capital markets brokers will have a good sense of who the "best" buyer is.

Sometimes, the owner and the capital markets broker will select two or three buyers to counteroffer. Another way to handle the last round is to call for a best-and-final offer from a smaller subset of the original.

Ownership will then select a buyer and go under contract. The broker collaborates with the buyer's team, including their attorneys, to facilitate due diligence. This means they will help the buyer evaluate the asset and validate the assumptions that were shared in the marketing package.

Finally, the transaction will close, and the broker will earn their fee. It can take many months to sell a building and years to build the relationship that allows the broker to get the listing.

Between selling buildings for active owners, the broker will stay in touch with owners most likely to transact. The broker frequently sends them market update reports that discuss sales price trends and other valuable information. This helps investors stay informed about market conditions, enabling them to make informed decisions about when to buy or sell assets.

In sum, capital markets brokers must pay close attention to detail and have a very deep financial background in commercial real estate analytics. They also need a deep understanding of investor motivations and the ability to accurately help someone understand why an asset would make sense for them. This can be a highly compensated yet complex form of brokerage. Only a few brokers in the industry rise to the top level of capital markets sales.

CHAPTER 4

Real Estate Broker Compensation

*"The way to get started is to quit talking and
begin doing."*—Walt Disney

How are brokers paid? We need to start with the type of brokerage service you provide. Recognizing that there are many specialty areas in commercial real estate, I will focus on the "big three": tenant rep, landlord rep, and capital markets. Additionally, for the purposes of this section, we will have a United States-centric conversation, as compensation practices differ in the rest of the world.

One more qualifier: fees vary by US market and even by transaction type. The fee discussion may be the subject of an intense negotiation. As a tenant rep, I usually have the discussion early and get the agreement memorialized with a formal commission agreement. Then I can get to work on the deal and serve the client.

Commercial real estate fees for most transactional brokers are earned when a transaction occurs, which could mean the lease is executed or a building sale agreement is completed. In the United States, the convention is that landlords typically pay brokerage fees on leasing transactions. However, there is no free lunch for the tenant or occupier as the cost of commissions is baked into the rent they pay.

In a building sale, the listing broker's fee is most often paid by the seller, although there can be exceptions, especially in very large building dispositions. If the buyer has a broker, then that broker is almost always required to look to their client for a fee.

The bottom line on compensation is that successful brokers are extremely well compensated.

There is another issue to consider in a commission sales environment. There is virtually no cost of goods sold to the broker (not the real estate company). My father used to run a land planning firm, and he had to pay millions of dollars in salaries every year. A friend of mine runs a large manufacturer. His company has salaries *and* raw materials that have to be paid for before the first nickel of profit is earned.

As a commercial real estate service provider, there may be a cost associated with hiring an analyst, and occasionally, a team will bear the burden of a salary. Additionally, there may be costs associated with conferences, sales training, technology/apps, and business development expenses. However, in most cases, team members receive a portion of the fee when deals happen, thus there's no real cost of goods sold apart from the few soft costs enumerated above.

When this business is done well, the best brokers can make movie star money.

Tenant Rep

When a lease is signed, the tenant rep adds up all lease payments due during the lease's initial term. This is referred to as the *total lease value* or *total consideration*. Next, the broker multiplies the total lease value by an agreed-upon percentage, which is likely to be somewhere between 4% and 5%. The resulting math is the "gross" fee due to the broker.

The broker will have a "split" of this gross fee with their employer (also referred to as the brokerage), which can range from 50% of the gross fee to as little as 10% or 20%. A "split" refers to the portion of the fee that goes to the brokerage house. The broker provides a workplace and support, among other things. They also need to make a living!

The broker's split is usually determined by a schedule that has levels of production. The more leasing you do in a year, the better the "split" will be in your favor. This bracketed approach works well both ways: senior people can make more money, and junior folks who don't have big production yet cost the brokerage less. Additionally, multiple brokers often work on a deal, each receiving their share of the commission.

To keep things simple, let's look at a transaction with one broker and a simple 50/50 split with the brokerage house.

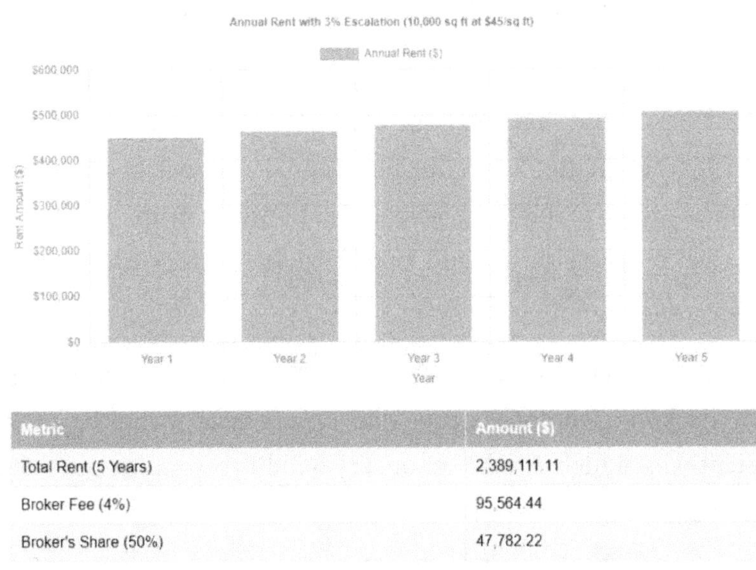

Metric	Amount ($)
Total Rent (5 Years)	2,389,111.11
Broker Fee (4%)	95,564.44
Broker's Share (50%)	47,782.22

This table summarizes the math for a 10,000 s.f. office lease at $45 per foot per year with a 3% escalation each year over 5 years. The broker's fee earned at 4% is just under $100,000, and after splitting with the brokerage house, the broker pockets just under $50,000.

For a 10,000-square-foot office lease at $45 per square foot per year with a 3% escalation each year over 5 years, the fee earned at 4% is just under $100,000. After your split with the brokerage house, you pocket just under $50,000 from a single transaction.

Do 10 or 20 deals this size, and pretty soon you are talking real money. Now you can see why this business is so sought after and so competitive. Millions of dollars annually will put some wind in your financial sails!

Landlord Representative

In most US markets, landlord representatives typically earn about 50% of what tenant reps earn on a given transaction. This pay structure reflects the nature of the roles. The tenant rep is hired to deliver a full-service solution, often resulting in a signed lease—a tangible outcome. In contrast, the landlord "lists" the building and often has an existing tenant they're trying to renew or replace, which can reduce the perceived risk on their side.

Landlord reps must first "win the listing," meaning they need to be selected by the building owner to represent the property. Once hired, their focus shifts to building strong relationships with tenant reps, conducting property tours, and preparing lease proposals to attract tenants.

While landlord rep roles may seem less risky, they can still be highly lucrative. I know landlord agents who earn a great living. If you can consistently list a high number of quality buildings, your income can be more stable, and the earning potential is significant.

In some cases, especially if you work directly for a building owner, you might be on a salary with a bonus structure. However, the majority of landlord reps work on a commission basis and are compensated through transaction-based fees.

Capital Markets Brokers

Capital markets brokers are the fighter pilots of commercial real estate. They are part of a very small community of brokers that sell the biggest assets for large real estate owners. These brokers often have to complete an extensive broker's opinion of value and create elaborate "pitches" to get hired. Of course, the relationships with key investors and owners can take years to develop. When they do win, capital markets brokerage fees can range from approximately 1-2% down to about 75 basis points. If they sell an asset for $250 million and earn 0.75%, then the fee is $1,875,000. Fees are market and deal-specific, of course.

The largest capital markets teams typically have salaried analysts on staff; however, if you sell a few large assets a year, it is easy to cover a few analysts at $125,000 or so per year.

Splits with Shops

When I think about commercial real estate brokerages ("shops"), I generally place them into three categories.

First, there are the large national and global firms, companies like Cushman & Wakefield, CBRE, and JLL. These are publicly traded firms with deep resources, broad service offerings, and strong brand recognition. They typically have in-house experts across different specialties, excellent marketing support, and extensive operational infrastructure. The trade-off is that individual brokers may receive a lower share of commissions, known as a lower split.

Next are the mid-sized firms, such as Colliers and Cresa, for example. These firms often operate under a partnership model. Local offices may be independently owned but connected to a larger national or international brand. Mid-sized firms offer many of the same benefits as larger firms, such as shared resources and name recognition, but with a bit more flexibility and often slightly better splits for the broker.

Lastly, there are local, independent brokerages that focus on a single market or a small region. These firms tend to be more entrepreneurial. They may have informal alliances with firms in other markets or rely on professional networks such as SIOR to share referrals. While they typically have fewer built-in resources and limited marketing support, they often offer significantly higher commission splits. Brokers in these firms tend to be more hands-on, handling a greater portion of their own marketing and operational work.

Each model has its strengths. Generally speaking, the bigger the firm, the more support and brand power you'll find, but with lower personal earnings per deal. The smaller the firm, the more independent you'll need to be, but the financial upside can be much higher.

	SHOP TYPE	COMMISSION TO BROKER %
●	Small	65 - 75
●	Mid	55 - 65
●	Big	50 - 55

Another consideration is a "stair step" of splits. Almost all brokerage firms start on a calendar-year basis with splits: the lowest to the broker and the highest to the shop. Then, as the broker closes deals—referred to as production in the business—the splits become more favorable to the broker.

Here's an example: In a mid-sized shop, the first tier of production might range from $1 to $150,000 in fees. That tier might be split at 55%

to the broker and 45% to the shop. The next tier might be $151,000-$250,000, and those splits could be 60% to the broker and 40% to the shop.

Here are some considerations as you think about selecting a type of brokerage to partner with:

1. Ask the managing principal or broker to provide the average production of a broker and offer some examples (without names) of what top brokers produce in a year. This will vary depending on the real estate cycle, but you can apply the splits to production levels and start estimating how much money you can make.

2. To make a broad generalization, large shops focus on big deals. Now, don't throw rocks at me! I know all shops can land large business opportunities. However, in my experience, the size of deals the bigs can secure is larger, in part, because of the perception of brand, safety, and experience.

3. What resources are available to help you prepare for pitches and deliver services in your area of interest? For example, if you want to be a tenant rep, does the brokerage pay for databases of companies and databases of buildings where your clients could take space? Does the brokerage have a customer relationship management system to help you track your leads? What else do they offer in technology, and will it cost you money?

4. Culture is everything, regardless of the shop's size. If you are being offered a position and are new to commercial real estate, ask to speak with others around your age and stage at the company. Try to get honest feedback on how things work in the shop. Review sites like Glassdoor and general social media platforms, which may provide valuable feedback. Finally, ask brokers you trust at other shops for their perception of the shop(s) you are considering joining.

5. Don't become so focused on splits that you forget benefits, mentorship, training, support, marketing, research, and all the services you will need to be successful. Consider creating a matrix to compare shops.

6. I love the idea of starting in research and then shifting to brokerage a year or two later. You get paid a salary to learn the market and can go to breakfast and lunch with everyone who will meet with you to learn. When you eventually become a broker, you will be loaded for bear!

7. I will cover this more specifically later, but if you are going to work at a particular firm, who will mentor and train you? Will you be working alone or as part of a team?

There is no perfect answer to selecting a brokerage, and in some sense, the decision may be made for you...The job opportunity you have in front of you!

CHAPTER 5

Occupier: Reasons Companies Lease Space

"Patience is the companion of wisdom."
—Saint Augustine

One key to being a broker serving the business community is an understanding of *why* companies need real estate. Companies do not lease real estate for the fun of it. They have a business imperative. For example, a client may be setting up an office in San Francisco to capitalize on the AI talent available in the marketplace.

Or perhaps they want to move their headquarters to a Sun Belt city like Atlanta, Dallas, or Charlotte to lower costs and attract top talent from great pools.

Your job is to know the why before the what. And, in conjunction with your senior broker, don't be afraid to ask questions and even (respectfully) challenge assumptions. Commercial real estate decisions are crucial for the company's success, and part of your job is to help the executives make the right decision.

A secondary issue is how corporations manage real estate; specifically, whether to lease or buy. In general, buying makes sense in only a few cases (more on this below): there is a high upfit for a lab or specialty manufacturing space, the company is massive and will be in the location for decades to come (think Google, Microsoft or Apple), or the company is near a specialized workforce (military contractors near a base).

If one is going to own the real estate, to me, the magic number is 20. If you are certain your company will remain in the asset and at the same size for 20 years or more, then the math supports putting your capital in the building.

For the vast majority of corporations, the most common method of controlling real estate is through leasing. Executives would quite simply invest their precious capital in the business, which might have a "hurdle rate" of return of 30% or greater against a real estate return of 10% or less.

Let's continue with a scenario. Imagine that you're the CEO of a mid-cap company with annual sales of $1 billion. Your workforce consists of knowledge workers, and your principal real estate is office space. Consistently, on an annual basis, your second-largest cost, after labor, is your facilities. A significant part of your role as CEO is to serve as a fund allocator. Where will you allocate your dollars to achieve the highest return on investment? Let's first look at the situation from an ownership perspective. What if you were to buy all of your company's real estate?

As we zoom in, here are some issues to consider when buying real estate for a company:

1. Availability of the right real estate in the right location to purchase.
2. Upfront capital required, which can certainly include debt. This introduces the risk of dealing with a lender.
3. Flexibility to outgrow the facility or to contract with the facility.
4. Multi-tenant versus single-tenant: It's unlikely that an operating business would buy a multi-tenant building because that puts them solidly in a different business, which is operating real estate. Therefore, they would need to find a single-tenant building that suits their needs.

5. Facility operational issues: If you own the building, you have to handle all the heartaches, including roof and structure maintenance, and all the costs and decisions related to upkeep.

So, given the above, what are other examples of companies that would buy real estate for their portfolio?

- Manufacturers with significant investments and difficult-to-move equipment.

- Specialized uses, such as data centers (especially for large companies).

- The largest companies in the world, such as Apple and Google, own substantial real estate portfolios. However, they are sophisticated in their approach and view real estate as a hedge and a component of their investment strategy. They also tend to cluster in campuses and expand and contract as the business needs to on a building-by-building basis within the campus.

- Very small companies, typically owned by a single individual. Owning real estate can be part of the company owner's wealth-building plan. This is the case with small CPA, Law, Investment, or Consulting firms. These entrepreneurs will spend their working lives in their company and, over 20-30 years, can achieve significant wealth in the reversion (sale) of their building when they close or sell their companies.

The net result is that most American companies will lease space. They can moderate their upfront costs and have much more flexibility to grow or contract their portfolios. Additionally, professional landlords can operate facilities much more efficiently than many companies that operate real estate with expert capabilities.

Leasing Considerations

Starting with office use, several critical factors come into play when companies look for leased premises. These considerations help ensure the space is cost-effective, functional, and scalable. Based on my experience, here are the key things companies typically look for, grouped into logical categories for clarity. This is not exhaustive, as detailed analyses can encompass up to nearly 100 specific factors; however, it focuses on the most commonly emphasized ones.

Location

- Proximity to employees, clients, and vendors to minimize commute times and enhance convenience.
- Accessibility via public transportation, major highways, and walkable areas.
- Surrounding amenities like restaurants, shops, and services that support employee satisfaction.
- Local business environment, including competition, zoning laws, and neighborhood safety.

Space Requirements and Layout

- Adequate size based on current employee count, with room for future growth (e.g., additional workstations or storage).
- Flexible layout options, such as open-plan designs, private offices, conference rooms, and communal areas.
- Alignment with company culture and work style, including natural lighting, ventilation, and ergonomic considerations.

Budget and Costs

- Total cost of occupancy, including base rent, utilities, property taxes, maintenance fees, and potential rent escalations.

- Hidden or additional expenses like security deposits, insurance, and tenant improvement allowances.
- Value for money, balancing premium features against overall affordability and long-term financial impact.

Lease Terms and Flexibility

- Length of the lease, renewal options, and clauses for early termination or subleasing.
- Negotiation leverage for favorable terms, such as rent abatements or expansion rights.
- Adaptability for business changes, such as short-term options or clauses that allow modifications to the space.

Amenities and Infrastructure

- Essential building features like high-speed internet, parking, elevators, and HVAC systems.
- Employee perks, such as gyms, kitchens, bike storage, or on-site cafeterias.
- Technology and utility readiness, including electrical capacity and cybersecurity measures.

Accessibility and Security

- Compliance with accessibility standards for people with disabilities (e.g., ramps, restrooms).
- Robust security features like 24/7 monitoring, access controls, and emergency preparedness.
- Parking availability, bike facilities, and low-traffic areas to ease daily operations.

Building Management and Reputation

- Quality of the landlord or property management team in terms of responsiveness and maintenance.
- Reviews and feedback from current tenants on building condition and service.
- Overall reputation of the building and landlord to avoid legal or operational risks.

Growth Potential and Fit-Out

- Scalability for business expansion, including options to add space or reconfigure layouts.
- Fit-out readiness—from basic shell spaces to turnkey setups— with allowances for customization.

Do Companies Lease Space After COVID? Why Don't We All Just Work from Home?

The pundits asked both during and after the COVID-19 pandemic: Will we just work from home forever?

It's a fair question.

We've learned a lot in the post-COVID era about how office space will be used moving forward. For centuries, people have gathered in physical workplaces to collaborate, innovate, and execute business. If you want to become a top-performing broker, whether on the landlord or tenant side, it's worth taking time to think carefully about why companies still choose to lease office space today.

A turning point in this shift happened on June 29, 2007, the day the first iPhone was released. Before then, most professionals had to go into the office because their work physically required it. Paper files, desktop computers, and landlines made remote work nearly impossible for many.

However, after 2007, digital tools began to emerge that enabled people to work from anywhere. However, deeply held beliefs and cultural obligations kept in-person work as the only option.

As technology marched ahead, more and more remote collaboration tools were introduced and improved almost monthly. For example, video meeting tools like Zoom, Teams, and others have developed increasingly robust feature sets. Also, in late 2010, travel by US knowledge workers reached record numbers, necessitating de facto remote communication.

COVID-19 accelerated what was already a growing trend. Practically overnight, remote work became the norm for millions, and companies had to adapt at scale.

I wrote an article called "Are We Giving COVID Too Much Credit?" that looked at this idea. In truth, the decline in office utilization—especially on Mondays and Fridays—had already started before the pandemic. COVID didn't invent remote work; it just pushed it into the mainstream.

Still, just as predictions about the death of physical retail were exaggerated, so are the claims that the office is finished. As Colin Connolly, CEO of Cousins Properties, put it: "Office is not obsolete—obsolete office is obsolete." I completely agree. Like cars or homes, preferences for office space are evolving rapidly.

One landlord I know put it this way: "It's not about the space anymore. It's about the place." In other words, office space must now offer something meaningful, something that brings people together with purpose.

So, why do employers continue to lease office space even when remote work is an option? The answer to that question could easily fill a book, but I'll summarize with four key reasons why the office still matters:

- Culture
- Accountability
- Learning
- Speed of business

Culture

"Culture is a concept that encompasses the social behaviors, institutions, and norms found in human societies, as well as the knowledge, beliefs, arts, laws, customs, capabilities, and habits of the individuals in these groups. Culture often originates from a specific region or location." - *Wikipedia*

A leader's approach to running their business relies on culture as a foundation. To illustrate, think about how you feel when you walk into a Home Depot store vs a Chick-fil-A. Both stores meet some of our needs, but the employees and environments are different.

The same is true in corporate America. I've toured hundreds of companies' offices, and I can tell a lot about their culture just by being in their physical spaces. So can employees and clients.

An office space can also play a significant role in sharing the company's values. When new employees arrive, companies sometimes literally put their values on the wall for all to see. The new hires get a sense of how seriously the company takes the values on display in a big way.

One other way culture and values are shared is through a "marketing walk" in the space. I've visited dozens of spaces that feature corporate museums and many others that showcase products for visitors to see. An executive will walk the client or prospect through the space, proudly sharing why their product is vastly superior to Brand X.

Accountability

The work needs to get done. You can debate me and tell me you will work hard at home. Maybe you are right. However, I think that when we're all physically in the same place, we have stronger accountability. I have reviewed surveys of large groups of knowledge workers. Many of them report fewer distractions at their offices (no dogs, laundry, kids, spouses, or other similar issues to deal with). Employers are paying real dollars for knowledge workers' services, and one key indicator of working hard is being present. As in, *in the office.*

Remember when you were in school and you had study groups? One purpose of the group was to encourage everyone to get the work done. The office is not that different, except that the boss is likely there!

Another issue is that in the office, a knowledge worker should have all the necessary tools to complete an assignment. Tech tools, whiteboards, advanced printing functions, and strong wifi all help get the worker tuned up to complete the study or prepare for the pitch!

Learning

When I was a new commercial real estate broker, one thing I wanted to do the most was sit in a senior broker's office and simply listen to them talk. I can still vividly remember some of the conversations I heard. In-person learning is significantly more effective than remote learning, especially for newer knowledge workers. If you're unsure, ask a kid who had to go to school remotely during COVID.

We learn when we listen, but we also learn from non-verbal cues. Watching how the boss or a senior performer carries themself is important. So is watching them work and think in an in-person meeting.

Finally, as you consume material in training or prepare to complete a work stream, having the ability to pop over and ask someone a question can help you process much more quickly AND build confidence in your work.

Speed of Business

Not long ago, I had lunch with the director of real estate of a very large company. He oversees one of the largest real estate portfolios in the world. We discussed the work-from-home vs. work-from-the-office debate. "We need our people back in the office for one simple reason: speed of business," he said.

I can spend days trying to set up a video meeting with a busy colleague, or I can catch them on the way in from lunch and solve a problem with a one-minute discussion. It's hard to replicate that conversation so quickly in a video meeting, and most executives get a HUGE number of emails, texts, Slack messages, and other communications. They simply cannot focus quickly on an issue unless you are in front of them.

At the end of the day, in any capitalist system, every investment must deliver a return. That includes commercial real estate.

As a successful broker, your job is to clearly explain why leasing or owning space is a smart business decision. You must be able to show how it supports a company's goals for growth, stability, and long-term success.

One way I stay sharp is by regularly meeting with executives and asking thoughtful questions about their hopes, concerns, and priorities. These conversations are invaluable. They provide insight that goes beyond market reports and headlines.

You need to think for yourself, but you also need to think strategically. Understand your market. Know your product. Be able to connect what you're offering to what business leaders truly care about.

When you can speak confidently with decision-makers about how their real estate investments align with their business objectives, you're not just selling space; you're speaking their language. And that's a big part of what will set you apart and lead you to long-term success.

Hustle as a Strategy

The day was April 17th, 1997, when I took an elevator ride that would change my life.

Mark Christopher was a very senior and well-respected broker at Cushman & Wakefield, and I was, well, I was wet behind the ears. I had been in the real estate business for less than two years, and I was banging my head against the wall, cold-calling small industrial tenants in a grungy Atlanta industrial submarket.

I was beginning to make some traction, but like so many young people in our business, I had a strong fear of failure and an unhealthy case of self-doubt.

We both walked to the office elevator right at 7:30 PM on that Thursday. I'm sure Mark had had a long day. At that time, I didn't know him personally, but I sure as heck respected his reputation. When we boarded the elevator, he looked right at me and asked how it was going. I said with a little too much enthusiasm, "Busy!"

Mark smiled and said with intensity, "Ken, but are you GOOD busy?" I didn't really know how to respond because I was working so hard, and I felt I was doing the right thing every day. I thought about the many administrative tasks I had done that day, and I stammered, "I'm not sure what you mean." The doors opened, and we got off the elevator.

He stopped in the lobby and again looked right at me with a brilliant smile and a piercing gaze and said, "Come by my office in the morning. 8:00 A.M. sharp."

Thus began a mentor relationship that completely retooled my way of thinking. I quickly transitioned from industrial tenant rep to office tenant rep. Mark let me sit in his office and just *listen* to him talk to clients. I was in heaven. His trust in me did wonders for my self-confidence.

His unwarranted kindness in spending time with me is something I think about often. I will strive to pay forward his investment in me for the rest of my life.

Fake Busy

In our short time together, I learned much from Mark Christopher, and I want to share two formative lessons here today.

On our first day together, Mark sent me a copy of a September 1986 Harvard Business Review Story entitled "Hustle as A Strategy." The article posited that, "...A vision is only as good as the energy, resourcefulness, and professionalism that combine to service every customer and every new opportunity every day."

As I've thought about this piece and Mark's wisdom over the years, I've learned to question myself about "Fake Busy" vs. "Good Busy."

Because we are performing a lot of tasks every day, and because we call ourselves busy does not mean we are being productive.

Clarity about where you are headed is essential so you can say "no" more often than you say "yes" to non-mission-critical tasks. Don't allow "fake busy" to give you comfort. Hustle in the wrong direction is not hustle at all. Plus, I think saying "no" is a true superpower that so many do not possess.

Provide Exceptional Service

The second lesson is simple on the surface: be a true service provider. Provide excellent, amazing service, and clients will remember. In a word: hustle. As a tenant rep, my mission is to help others with theirs, with a huge bias towards action.

Here are four specific things that I focus on in client relationships:

1. **The digital nod.** I acknowledge clients' emails within half a day, even if I need to work to get an answer. They are trusting us with an important relationship, and I want them to know I am listening and responding as quickly as humanly possible.
2. **Call them before they call you.** When working on an assignment, I don't want the client to have to call me to ask how things are going. I call them frequently when we have meaningful updates to report. Sometimes I just call to chat and say hello. Relationships matter.
3. **Do the lifting.** Manage the meeting notes or offer to create presentations for more senior management and boards of directors. Deliver value by supporting the client.
4. **When sending proposals and financial runs, I work to give an honest opinion as to what the data means.** They are hiring you because you are an expert; so, share your expert opinion.

In short, the client should be delighted to work with you. We have done our jobs when our client gets bonused, promoted, or complimented internally. It's all about our hustle to help them with their hustle.

Planning is great, but <u>hustle and massive action are required</u> to win a football game or develop a true business relationship.

A postscript: Sadly, Mark Christopher died a year after our elevator ride from an aggressive form of cancer. He was 42. He left behind a wife, two kids, and a devastated mentee. I think of him often. And I try to honor his memory by repaying his investment in me to those early in their careers.

Helping others is hustle, too. And I know I have a sacred duty to do so.

I hope Mark can somehow hear this, and I hope he is smiling his brilliant smile. Mark, I am trying hard to be GOOD busy. Every. Single. Day.

SECTION TWO

On Getting Hired

The Roadmap to Getting Hired in Commercial Real Estate Brokerage. Going From Your Couch to Your New Gig!

"As iron sharpens iron, so a friend sharpens a friend."
—King Solomon

It may seem daunting. It certainly did to me. How do you get someone to meet with you, to listen to you, to have confidence in you, and then to hire you to work in their commercial real estate brokerage?

Like anything big in life, you take it one step at a time. The old saying: "How do you eat an elephant? One bite at a time."

This section breaks the process into manageable, actionable pieces.

First, some programming notes: We can start creating your custom *Real Estate Prescription.* See Appendix 1 for the worksheet. Print the worksheet out or load it on your tablet for a soft copy. Feel free to use tools such as Evernote to create a custom document.

As you read each part of this Section 2, begin to create your own prescription. You must capture your initial "to-dos" as you read the material. Once you complete Section 2 and have a full prescription, you can change, reduce, or modify as your thoughts about how to enter commercial real estate change. The bottom line is, now is the time to capture what and how you will execute your own prescription.

Let's get started!

Create a Business Plan That Will Impress

When trying to get hired as a broker, it helps to have something to sell other than your wonderful personality and great looks. You should have a business plan (sometimes called a business development plan).

"How do I generate a plan if I have never been in the business?" you might rightly ask. We will have several versions in this book, and you can select the one that interests you.

Before we get to the types of plans, let's discuss some general keys to success. A very successful friend of mine starts sales meetings with the following phrase: "Who will do what by when?" This accountability statement is strong. As I sometimes ask, "What's the verb? Who is going to make it happen here?"

1. **You are trying to secure yourself and your future team, hired to provide professional services.** Your plan will change. Don't overthink the plan. The best plan is the one you have created. However, writer's block can overwhelm. Just get something on paper. If you know other brokers, you can ask them to review it. Alternatively, look for a Council of Young Realtors or other "for under-30s" professional organizations in your area and reach out. You can also ask friends who are in sales or other professions. Refer to the helpful plan examples and links in Appendix 2 for guidance.

2. **Make the plan short.** No executive wants to read a 30-page plan. I'd say three to five pages is ideal. A reminder that my lens is one

of a tenant rep. If you are trying to become a landlord or capital markets broker, adjust to their (and their clients') perspective.

A sample layout could be:
  i. Area or focus
  ii. Target executive (also called an "avatar")
  iii. Understand the executive's worries and needs.
  iv. The ability to address the executive's concerns with the brokerage team you are trying to join. Read senior brokers' LinkedIn profiles to see what strengths they highlight.
  v. Tactics for reaching out: How will you get in front of an executive?
  vi. Goals for those tactics. How many calls, posts, emails, etc.?
  vii. How will you record your activity? You can use something as simple as a spreadsheet. It does not have to be complex.
  viii. What is your accountability function? Will you report to your senior broker every Friday by 3:00 p.m., for example?
  ix. How long will the campaign last? Six months? A year?
  x. How will you know if you've been successful? For example, "I will make 50 contacts a week over six months, which is 1,300 calls." When you are successful 3% of the time, that is 39 meetings. Of the 39 meetings, you convert 10%—just under 4 transactions.

3. Your plan does not need to be original. Football teams run the same plays week after week. However, it must be probable that you can actually pull it off. Be reasonable about the number of calls you are going to make, for example. I want to give you

permission to review others' plans and adapt them as your own. You can't wholesale copy, but you can certainly reuse ideas and then personalize them.

Here are four typical business development approaches for a tenant representative who is focused on one area of a city or community:

1. **Submarket**
    - In a submarket-focused business development plan, the broker selects a specific submarket within the city to focus on. Selection can be based on several criteria, such as choosing the largest submarket or the one with a cool, growing area.
    - Next, use common commercial real estate databases to identify all tenants and begin locating the decision-making executive.
    - As mentioned earlier, consider the executive's common challenges (high rental rates, insufficient space, troublesome landlords, etc.) and outline how you plan to address them in your outreach.

2. **Radius**
    - If you are trying to join a team and you see they've done a large deal in the past year or so in a particular building, then you can set a radius around that building of blocks or miles, depending on the size and density of the location. New York City would be blocks, Dallas would be, say, a mile in any direction. To determine big deals your prospective team has worked on, try searching their names along with the local business journal, which may have written about them. Or you can simply ask!

3. **Vertical**
    - Select an industry vertical, such as law, accounting, or technology, and identify all the companies within that sector. Visit industry association trade sites and identify the problems the industry faces that could be addressed by real estate. For example, in

professional service firms, returning to the office after COVID continues to be a major issue. Would a cool new office building help get young workers back? Now you have a solution to sell!

4. **Size**
   - Start with a certain tenant size. I have a friend who has been in the business for many years but focuses on 5,000-square-foot tenants. He is the "king of small," and they love him for it. He makes many hundreds of thousands of dollars a year by focusing (and telling the market that he focuses) on their occupancy size. Select the size range you want to start on. Smaller tenants are typically easier to reach, and there is less competition from other, more experienced brokers.

How to Get a Meeting with Prospective Brokerages and Whom to Meet

Time to get your calendar full and grip and grin! You need to meet with brokerages to attempt to get hired. Where do you start? First, let's be clear that you are trying to set up a meeting to learn about the commercial real estate industry and/or to get a job. We are not selling washing machines here. Knowing the focus of your meeting in advance is important. I tell young folks to make the first three to five meetings with real estate professionals "advice" meetings, where you ask the executive for advice about how they started their career and how you can start yours.

Meetings after that can certainly include advice questions, but the focus is on building a relationship that can lead to a job opportunity. You are "hunting" in the sense that you are laser-focused on finding an opportunity or a job opening.

Figure Out the Playing Field

Determine the commercial real estate shops in town. You can do this task in several ways. You can use your local business journal's "book of lists," or you can ask a friend in the business. If you are using technology beyond Google searches, consider checking out CoStar or LoopNet. Increasingly, AI tools can help with these types of searches. Finally, your local commercial board of realtors or chamber of commerce may have lists.

Next, visit the website or LinkedIn profile of the firms you'd like to meet with. Determine who the managing principal or CEO of the office is. Pull them up individually on LinkedIn and see if you have any first or second-level connections in common. If you do, you can reach out to those individuals and ask for an introduction.

Database tools like Apollo and ZoomInfo can help you find almost any business person's email and cellphone number. They are not free, but they are super powerful.

Also, try to identify the top teams in town. Many commercial real estate boards publish an annual list of top producers. If you are unsure where to find this information, simply call the CEO of the local board and ask. If you don't have a mutual connection, then you can practice your "direct contact" skills. I don't believe in "cold calls." Instead, I research someone and reach out with a "value proposition." How do you have a value proposition if you have never had a job? Determine the needs and wants of the person you are calling on. You don't have to know them at all. You can create an "avatar" of who the buyer would be.

Let's give it a shot.

The typical "buyer" of commercial real estate talent (a broker or leader of an office) in City X is 45-55 years old, has 5-10 years of tenure, is rushing from meeting to meeting, and answers a ton of emails. They work very hard, and their greatest desire is to recruit new brokers to expand their business. These ideal broker candidates are organized in their prospecting data, disciplined in their outreach, fearless on the phone, and great at building relationships.

If you have friends in the business, you can "workshop" this approach with them. Additionally, general businesspeople will work on this task, especially if they regularly enter into purchase agreements on behalf of their company. Ask them to visualize themselves running a sales organization.

The key is first to determine the needs of the person who will be picking up the phone or responding to the email. Most job seekers get this all wrong and focus on themselves. They are really net *takers*... "Can I have a meeting? Can I have an offer? Can I have a job?" Instead, be a net *giver*, and you will get hired and go far in sales.

Let's draft the script of a phone call with our avatar, Mr. Mason. Mr. Mason answers:

"Hi, this is Jennie Smith, and I'm a recent graduate of the University of High Achievers with a degree in Business. I've read many books on commercial real estate and developed a prospecting plan for the CBD office market. I would appreciate the opportunity to schedule a few minutes to discuss your advice and feedback on the plan. May I suggest some times for a meeting?"

Some things to note about the script. You did not ask for a job interview, and in the last sentence, you didn't even ask for the meeting! You asked if you could send *times* for a meeting. I refer to this approach as asking the *minimum viable question, or "MVQ."*

Why ask a closing question in this way? Because executives often have decision fatigue, asking them to commit time to someone new to the industry is harder for them to answer than "Can I suggest some times for a meeting?" The "times" question is fundamentally an easier "ask" because they haven't fully committed to the meeting.

When they say *yes*, have three options ready immediately. You can ask them to check right then. It's a little pushy, but if you email the executive, I bet you a cheeseburger you will never hear back. When they select one, offer to send the invitation. You are the one requesting the meeting. Include your cell phone number in the invite, so they can contact you quickly if they have a conflict.

Thank them, then hurriedly get off the phone. Why? One of the many errors someone can make in sales is to keep talking after the sale (in this case, they agreed to a meeting). Salespeople feel euphoria when they get a "yes" and start running their traps. You can turn a *'yes'* into a *'no'* with the wrong comment.

You got the meeting, so move on. Congratulations, by the way! I'm proud of you in advance.

Dealing with Voice Mail: The Concept of Small Promises

It happens every hour of every business day, millions of times. Your call to a decision maker rolls to voicemail. I have a way to get through that requires nothing of your prospect. It's called the *concept of small promises*, and it works like this:

"Ring ring!" Voicemail. "Hi! This is Jessica Lambert, and I'm sorry I've missed you. I will try to call you back on Thursday at 2:30!" Click.

There are several things to note about this message. First, you did not say why you were calling, because it doesn't matter to the decision maker, and they could delete your message before they listen to it all. Secondly, the message is super brief and straight to the point. Thirdly, *you didn't ask the prospect to do anything*! Finally, you did not leave your phone number. At the very least, this message will make you stand out. When you call them back at 2:30 on Thursday, they may still not answer, but you are building trust. The next time they don't answer, leave a very similar message, but do so first thing in the morning. Change the time of day and day of the week with each message.

After the fifth message of this type, change it up.

"Hi Bob! This is Jessica Lambert. I will also email this to you to make your life easier. May I ask you to ring me at 912-123-4567? I would be grateful for no more than three minutes of your time."

It is much more likely that Bob will respond to your email or actually call you because you have built trust with small promises.

Trust me. This works.

Dealing with DM's and Text

We are living in a digital world. It is SO easy to block supplicants from reaching you in this arena.

The first rule in digital is to pick a channel and stick with it. If you are going to text, stay there. If you plan to DM (direct message) on LinkedIn, stick with it for at least a few weeks.

Keep your messaging *very* short. Think under 30 words. Your "call to action" is the same as above: "May I contact your EA to schedule a meeting?" or "May I suggest some times for a 15-minute call?"

Here are some subjects that you can use in the initial electronic message:

- **Praise:** Congratulations on your award/profits/big deal/new hire/merger/long career.

- **Advice:** I have an idea for a niche I would like to explore in commercial real estate. May I share it with you?

- **An event:** I see you will be attending the XYZ event (sometimes, lists are public). I would love to shake your hand and say hello for five minutes. (By the way, once you've reached your target, *then* you'll close the deal for the actual meeting, which is scheduled for a week or two later.)

- **Shared Social Club or School:** "I see we are both members of a college fraternity or sorority/same college/ same social club (parents' clubs count)/ same church or religious institution. May I suggest a few times to meet for coffee?"

Key to getting successful meetings through digital reach-outs:

1. Short messages.
2. Check your grammar so that it is perfect. You can run your messages through AI if you like.
3. Make sure you spell their name correctly every time!
4. Don't shorten names. Robert is not automatically Rob. When in doubt, use their last name and an honorific, such as Mr. or Ms.
5. Communicate once a week, for as long as it takes.
6. Shift the time and day of your reach-outs. I like Tuesday/ Wednesday/Thursday and shift from super early in the morning to early evening.

Don't lose hope. Eventually, they will see your note, and with repetition, they will be worn down. I know; I've been on the receiving end myself!

CHAPTER 7

Setting the Stage: Research and Preparation for the Interview

"The greatest danger for most of us is not that our aim is too high and we miss it, but that it is too low and we reach it." —Michelangelo

Congratulations, you got the meeting with a hiring manager. Now what?

"Everyone's in sales, whether they know it or not" is the old saying. When you are interviewing to become a commercial real estate broker, you KNOW you are headed into sales! The first thing you have to sell is yourself.

To be the most impressive you can be, you have to do research or "due diligence" on the person you are meeting with. We will start micro and go macro:

1. Read the individual's company resume and note tenure, specialty, awards, and leadership positions.
2. Review social media sites like LinkedIn for bio information, previous companies, interests, and hobbies. You should also specifically note if you have connections in common on LinkedIn.

3. Read about the top producers in the shop. You can usually find articles about them in local business journals or on their social media platforms. Study the winners.

4. Read all about the company. When was it started? What types of business does it chase? Is there a mission/vision/values? If so, study them!

5. Can you find deal announcements in the business journal or on the company's own marketing materials? Who are their major clients, and what services does the brokerage provide for them?

6. Has the company announced any growth plan, and if so, in what area?

Based on the above, you should develop at least five sharp questions. These questions are designed to let the leader know that you know about THEM, their accomplishments, their aspirations for growth, and how they are successful in their career.

I want you to write your own, but let's list five questions for your interview at Big Time Brokers, which is led by John Big Time and is publicly traded:

1. John, I see you started as a tenant rep 22 years ago. How did you break into the marketplace, and how did you become successful?

2. I know you've led the shop for the past five years; what is your leadership style?

3. What does Big Time Brokers do to support their top performers and make them even more successful?

4. I read about your mission/vision/values and love the approach. How do these statements play out in the culture at Big Time Brokers?

5. What are your growth plans for Big Time Brokers?

Take notes. Let me say that again. Take notes. On a paper pad. Listen carefully. You must be totally focused on John Big Time and let him know that you recognize his success. He should see you as a chip off the old block, wanting to become a mini John.

The reason I want you to take notes on a pad has nothing to do with technology. I'm pro-technology and love any kind of app or device that can save time. First, the paper pad shows respect; second, the decision maker can see you taking notes; and third, typing on a keyboard is distracting to the speaker.

As an aside, I am fine with you using an AI note-taking app during interviews. In most cases.

The final piece of preparation before the meeting is to consider how you will describe yourself and your life's successes so far. I hope you have at least three stories in your back pocket to break out as needed.

Here are some common themes:

1. Name a life issue that you have overcome and talk about how you did it. Did you have a health issue, did your parents divorce, did you move a lot, or did you overcome some huge issue to either get into or graduate from school?

2. Tell a sales story, no matter how small. Did you sell the most fruit on the football team or the band? Did you help your siblings in their efforts in some way? Did you start a small business, like cutting lawns and selling services?

3. Athletic success is a sure winner. Did you have a leadership role on your team in school, and did the team do great things? How did you contribute?

4. Community service is also a great opportunity to talk about yourself. Did you join a junior board or committee and execute on a project or raise money? How did your success help others, and what did you learn from it?

Stories are marvelous and help people get to know you and even become your fans. Everyone likes a good story of hard luck overcome by hard work.

My favorite book on storytelling is *Storyworthy* by Matthew Dicks. Storyworthy is a guide to crafting compelling personal stories, offering practical techniques for finding, shaping, and delivering narratives that captivate audiences.

Please pick up a copy and give it a read.

Ace the Meeting: The Ask for Advice Approach

The day has arrived, and you are ready for your meeting! Let's start with some housekeeping issues that will help destress you and build your confidence:

1. Call the receptionist or an assistant a few days in advance to let them know you have an interview scheduled. Ask them how your interviewer will dress that day, and mirror them as closely as possible.
2. Ensure your grooming and attire are top-notch.
3. Confirm the meeting by email the evening before.
4. Confirm you know the directions and where to park.
5. Take your ID with you in case you need to clear security.
6. Arrive 30 minutes early. You can review your notes in your car, then walk in at least 15 minutes early. This is helpful because you are there and can relax about the commute to the interview.
7. Be nice to the receptionist. Focus on them and ask about their day. Small talk helps make a good impression. I've been to pitches before where the CEO asks the receptionist (afterward) what they think about brokers/salespeople. You never know. Being nice is just the human thing to do AND good business.

8. While waiting, look at your notes, not your phone. There are too many negative impressions that can occur if you are staring at your phone, scrolling. Plus, it's distracting.

9. We need to discuss phones specifically. You can take them to the meeting, but put them in airplane or silent mode. Do not put them on the table. Keep them in an attaché case, purse, or another bag. Of course, do not look at them during the meeting unless you are looking for data relevant to the discussion.

When the interviewer walks out to meet you, stand confidently and smile. Look them directly in the eyes and deliver a firm handshake. Deliver a socially acceptable greeting like, "It's such a pleasure to meet you. I've been really looking forward to this meeting."

The first 90 seconds are the most important in your meeting. Executives "thin slice" as do all humans, and they are making an initial "like or not" decision quickly. In a first meeting, I usually decline the offer of a beverage unless it is right in front of me, as fulfilling the request can be a distraction.

Let them welcome you in. Then, you have a few options for what to do next. If they control the meeting, then let them talk. Pull out your paper pad and take notes.

When you start talking, you could begin by saying, "I looked at your LinkedIn profile and see we know such and such in common," or "we both went to the same school," or "grew up in the same area." You are trying to find a common bond. If you cannot find this commonality in advance, then simply ask them about the office you are in and how long they've been located there. Or ask them about an interesting piece of furniture or an award.

Once the meeting gets going, and they start asking you questions, I suggest you repeat the question back to give yourself time to think. You can pause for a moment before answering, then do your best to respond. Importantly, keep the answer short and to the point.

As the two of you get into the central part of the meeting, keep a few principles in mind:

Practice the 70/30 principle. 70% of the talking is done by the other person. When they are talking, you are winning.

Ask. For. Advice. Executives in their 40s/50s and 60s have many hard-luck stories. Work on the questions discussed earlier in this chapter, and be prepared to ask real-time questions based on their responses, along with any follow-up questions. Here's an example:

Mr. Big Time: "We have 70 brokers in this office, and this is the best office in the company."

You: "It's very impressive what you've built here. How did you do it? How do you recruit the best people?"

When you ask leadership-focused questions, you are placating their ego but also moving yourself up several levels. You are focused on them, their success, and how they will grow their business. The focus on you can come later.

As the meeting comes to a close, you should have a call to action (next steps) planned. The interviewer may direct this, but if they do not, have something planned. The call to action (also called a closing question) can be as simple as you saying, "May I follow up in three weeks? I'll tell you whom I've met since our meeting and share my latest version of a business development plan."

Watch the body language. Sometimes it's clear a meeting is over from the dialogue, and most executives are good at bringing things to a soft landing. Some common body language signs that a meeting is over:

Packing up, "washing" legs with an open hand, shifting feet, looking at a watch, or an iPhone. You get the idea. A great book on nonverbal communication is *What Every Body Is Saying* by Joe Navarro (a retired FBI special agent and master interrogator). I recommend it.

When the meeting is over, keep eye contact, smile, and shake hands again. Express your thanks and confidently stride towards the door. Remember to be nice to the receptionist again on your way out. Do not ask for parking validation unless it is offered. Otherwise, wave goodbye and hit the elevator.

A few final points to consider when leaving meetings. I say nothing until I'm in my car. If you are in the building lobby and jump on the phone to start discussing your meeting, you never know who might overhear and misunderstand your candid comments. Also, as soon as I get in the car, I voice dictate to Evernote (or use your preferred method) everything I can remember about the meeting in real-time. The flow, the questions, the art in the office, the interviewer's dress, and any personal details they shared. I usually keep thank-you notes in my car and handwrite them ASAP. You can address them later, but if the conversation is very fresh, your note will be authentic. Congratulations. You did it! You had a great interview.

However, we are just getting started on this pursuit.

CHAPTER 8

Long Term Low Pressure Follow Up: Make Them Remember You, Pro Style

"The fortune is in the follow-up." —Jim Rohn

The hardest thing to do is to get the first meeting. The second hardest thing to do is to have them remember you after the meeting. The key to success is in the follow-up strategy. This strategy begins *before* the meeting. Return to the research that you did before the meeting (page 88). You are searching for a follow-up theme. Ideally, this theme is something that you and John Big Time have in common. For example:

- You both went to the same school,
- You played the same sport,
- You were in the same organization as kids (think Scouts),
- You are passionate about the same hobby,
- You belong to the same club,
- You attend the same religious institution.

These themes may be discovered in real time during the meeting or through your research of an individual's social media postings. Another way to find a common theme is by asking a mutual friend.

Next, you are going to "touch" John Big Time at least three times before you ask for the next meeting. To be clear, all these touches are made via

US Mail (or hand-delivered if mail is slow in your area). Why? Because executives are overwhelmed with email, and DM's feel invasive. Also, we get less and less "real" mail these days. You will stand out with a letter.

First, send him a thank-you note the same day of your meeting (as referenced above).

Secondly, in about 10 days, send him a short note attached to a magazine article you "happened" to come across regarding one of those themes. Let's say you and John Big Time love to fish. Google the type of fishing and find an article you think would make him smile. Jot a handwritten note that says, "Thought of you when I saw this." Hope you are well." Importantly, there is no "ask" in this follow-up. You are simply reminding John Big Time that you exist.

In another 10 days, search for an article that has a positive spin on something having to do with commercial real estate. Ideally, in one of the business lines that John Big Time is responsible for. Of course, if you can find some media where John Big Time is quoted, that would be spectacular. However, an optimistic piece on the business will do fine as well.

Attach a similar note to the commercial real estate piece that might say, "I've been paying attention to the <blank> business line that you mentioned in our meeting. I am glad to see the momentum in your business. I've had several conversations since our meeting, and I will reach out in hopes of getting some advice on my latest business plan."

There. You've done it. You've set the stage to ask for advice again, and you've introduced the idea that you will reach out. As mentioned in the "How to Get a Meeting" section, you should either reach out to John Big Time's assistant or email him with a brief email suggesting three times when you could visit his office for 30 minutes or less. If he doesn't respond, try emailing him on a different day, early in the morning. I am a fan of Tuesday, Wednesday, and Thursday emails between 6:30 and 7:30 AM. It is fine to set the email to automatically deploy, but if he responds, you should send a reply very quickly. In other words, you need to be awake!

Keep reaching out every 10 days with different messages until he responds. Always be polite and brief. Your hustle will become apparent! One final thought: when you do get the meeting scheduled, be very respectful of time. At 29 minutes in, thank John Big Time for his time and note, "We are at the end of the time you committed to." He may invite you to continue to stay, but this shows that you value him and his time.

Staying in touch, politely, has a huge ROI. I've made my living doing it!

Managing Relationships: The Meet Sheet Is Your Relationship Radar

Years ago, I met a young person in a coffee shop, and I could tell he was the real deal. He had good gab, asked amazing questions, and listened actively. Then he did something that rocked me. He pulled out a printed spreadsheet and smiled. "What's that?" I asked. He had me. "This is a record of everyone I've met thus far, when I met them, and some notes about what I learned from them."

I thought this simple device was brilliant for a number of reasons. First, he created a little excitement in me to see who else he was meeting with. When I examined the document, my appraisal of *him* increased because of the other people he had met for coffee. Next, I saw that he was organized and could track his meetings and the pearls of wisdom they yielded. It gave me the feeling that he was listening to me, and I immediately wondered what would be written next to my name. Finally, I knew he would go on to meet with others in my town's real estate community. My name would be on the list. He was helping my "brand" in a small way by waving the list in front of others. So, the "prop" of keeping the list and physically having it present in the interview worked. There was also real value to the candidate from creating this document. I coined the term "Meet Sheet."

The *Meet Sheet* is essentially a flat file CRM (customer relationship management) document. When you are just getting started, tracking, say, 20-50 executives, doesn't require a very sophisticated CRM, such as Salesforce or Microsoft Dynamics. Your learning on CRMs should occur after you are in a shop.

You can customize your document to show follow-up activities with each candidate. You can also track your overall activity. "I had 12 meetings in the past 30 days, have written 20 letters, and made 50 phone calls" is a nice report. This type of data also helps maintain high self-confidence, which is absolutely necessary at this stage of your life!

Finally, the Meet Sheet serves as a record of who you met with and what you learned. This journal bears review and study. When you finally do get a job, load everyone into your real CRM and stay in touch. You never know when you will need to dust off some of those relationships!

CHAPTER 9

I Got an Offer Letter! What Should I Do Next?

"Time is the most valuable thing a man can spend."
—Theophrastus

First, congratulations! You've worked hard to get an offer letter — or two or three. I'm proud of you. We are not done yet, however. There are 11 areas I'd like you to consider before shaking hands and firing up your new computer. You can create a spreadsheet to evaluate all 11 areas. Devise a scale of one to five, with five meaning you are 100% happy with what the firm is offering, and one meaning totally unhappy. This way, you can codify your review and compare multiple firm offers, should that issue arise.

1) Compensation/Performance: What are your splits, of course (see splits section on page 57), but also, is your potential new firm willing to give you a small salary for six months or a year as you try to build your book of business? How will your performance be evaluated? Is your production or the amount of commissions generated the sole issue, or are you required to do well in other areas? For example, do you have to contribute a certain number of deal comparables to a research database? Just know the bogey so you can prepare yourself to succeed.

Some firms will offer a "draw," which is a loan against future production. Can this be guaranteed by a senior broker? Can the draw be forgiven if you achieve a certain production level? Does the draw have interest, and is it reasonable? When does the draw have to be paid back, and what happens if you cannot meet that schedule? How are expenses such as travel, business development meals and entertainment, mileage, etc, to be handled? You may have to pay for all of these yourself, but it is good to be aware of and budget for them. Is there an existing account or piece of business you can work on to help get you some level of income at the beginning?

Finally, can you invest a portion of your commissions in deals the house may be working on? For example, some brokerage shops employ a group investment strategy, in which brokers can pool their funds to participate in a deal. I know you're eager to cash your first commission and enjoy that big dinner, but wealth building should start as soon as possible!

2) Benefits: You may be healthy as a horse, but you still need insurance. Review the firm's packages and understand your cost share. Health, dental, and pet insurance are all good to ask about. Does the firm offer short and long-term disability insurance? These can be key if you become disabled, which, of course, can happen at any age.

3) Team Dynamics/Mentorship Commitment: Before you commit to working on a team, I recommend spending some time out of the office together. Go to a ball game or a dinner together. What does your spidey sense say about the team members? Does this feel right? You will be spending a lot of your waking hours with these people. It's good if you like or at least respect them.

Mentorship is almost more important than money in your first gig. Almost. You should create a mentorship plan in conjunction with your assigned mentor. The book *Mentoring Programs That Work* by Jenn

Labin is a great read for those looking to design something. Put it all on paper and ask the senior leader to sign and commit to the time. If you join without a clear commitment from your mentor, you will be disappointed. Also, don't forget the power of reverse mentorship. Is there something you can help *your* mentor with? LinkedIn profile, social media expertise, and new technology tools are all common answers to this question.

4) Culture and Brand: Above, we talked about the dynamics of your team or department. Now we must evaluate the firm-wide culture. Some of this evaluation will be based on your observation of how people interact. Does it feel positive and supportive or like a high-pressure situation? Read the mission/vision/values on the website and see if you can determine if they are reflected in the office. You can use online tools like Glassdoor to perform a basic reputation audit. Additionally, review the company's social media posts and those that tag the company. You can ask the company if they have evaluated their Net Promoter Score. I occasionally type into a basic internet search "xyz company is terrible" or a similar phrase, and see if folks are complaining about the company. Yes, you can take internet complaints with a pinch of salt, but it is good to know.

The company's brand perception in the marketplace is particularly important. Soon, the company's brand will be part of *your* brand. One of the best ways to validate a brand's quality is simply to ask others outside the company. If your parents are in the business world, ask them to reach out to their friends. Ask others you've met in the industry what they think. Write it all down. If you hear only good, that's a good sign, of course. If someone spills the beans on an issue, keep it in context. If the issue is serious enough (fired by a major client, a lawsuit, or a major departure by a team), ask leadership about the issue and how they explain it externally.

I want you to be proud of the company you are working for and feel great about the brand on your business card. Put in the work here.

5) Toolkit, Technology, and Office Space: What kind of technology stack will the firm offer you? Some common tools to ask about: CRM/Lead Management, marketing, email tools, data warehouse (for leases, etc.), communications tools like Teams or Zoom, and a real estate database of buildings in your area. Does the firm utilize AI that you can use to analyze client documents, such as draft leases? (In "regular" AI, everything becomes public when entered, so you cannot put client docs there. You need private AI domains.)

Where will you sit, and would you have the flexibility to move around to a quieter area if you need to read a lease or make an important phone call? Are there video tools available? As a knowledge worker, ensure you have all the necessary tools to create an efficient and effective work stream.

6) Research: Most brokerages have professionals whose full-time job is to provide market research support. They perform data collection and produce market analysis to help the brokers and their clients understand market conditions and trends. They should also be available to assist brokers in providing custom research as projects require it. One easy way to determine the capabilities they can provide is to ask for a meeting with the head of research and ask them to tell you about their team and how they support brokers. You are splitting your income with the company and "paying for" services. Research is one of the most important.

7) Training: One might assume that a company provides training on how to perform a job function. One could be wrong. Does the brokerage you are considering offer formal training, and if so, can you preview the materials (to check for quality and hopefully the comprehensive nature of the training)? Check how often the training is offered, and confirm there is no cost to you to attend. If there is no training, this is not necessarily a deal killer. Determine if the broker will support sending you to trade associations such as CCIM or SIOR, and whether they would pay or split the training cost with you.

Lastly, numerous third-party training options are available. For example, LinkedIn Learning has a huge database of courses. My friend Rod Santomassimo at The Massimo Group is another outlet. You may need to work with the broker to curate your own external training. Just do it.

8) Administrative and Marketing Support: If you are very young, you may feel funny using administrative support. A common misconception is that if you are very new (and young), you have to do everything yourself. You DO need to recognize your position in the firm and understand that others' projects will likely be prioritized over yours. However, knowing what kind of support is available will help you evaluate the firm. As you grow in tenure and production, using an administrative support worker will help you become more productive. Do you have access to an administrative professional? If so, what is their workload? Will they be allowed to help you put together property surveys and tools?

In terms of marketing and business development, some firms put all that work onto the administrative team. Others have separate marketing departments. If you can, ask to see examples of the firm's "pitch decks" to better understand its capabilities.

Does the firm have a stable of past pitches you can review and use to create your own?

9) The Firm's General Resources: By "general resources," I mean how many types of brokerage does the firm have? Do they perform office, industrial, data center, retail, and land, for example? Do they sell buildings, also known as capital markets? Do they provide consulting services?

It is important to know for two reasons. First, you may be able to refer opportunities you pick up in the community to experts in other verticals and get paid a referral fee. Second, it's important to understand the tools at your disposal to serve your clients. For example, I refer a lot of work to project management, which helps build out space, and workplace consulting, which helps firms create the right kind of office for them.

10) Support for Your Business Plan or Vice Versa: Remember that business plan you created? Well, now you are about to implement. If there is "cognitive dissonance" between you and your team on your plan, this can create a major issue. Take the time to review your plan with the leader to whom you will report, obtain their endorsement, and secure their sign-off. The same is true for your team.

Importantly, establish success metrics and regular reporting. You need to keep yourself on track and be able to report on your work. Remember, it can take a good while to get deals going, and you want your higher-ups to have a way of knowing how hard you are working.

11) Schedule: You will spend many of your waking hours at this gig. It's best to know what they expect, especially in a post-COVID world. I love working in the office. I also love not being in the office on Friday afternoon. Ask about general expectations for yourself so you can comply. Then exceed them. The early bird does get the worm.

This is a graphical example of your evaluation of the capabilities of the brokerages you are considering. Taking the time to do a deep dive and your best "look" into the various options will help you (a) make the best choice for you and (b) know that after you start, you made a data-based decision. Your brokerage choice is crucial to your success, and you will operate with immense confidence knowing you've chosen the best option for you in your market.

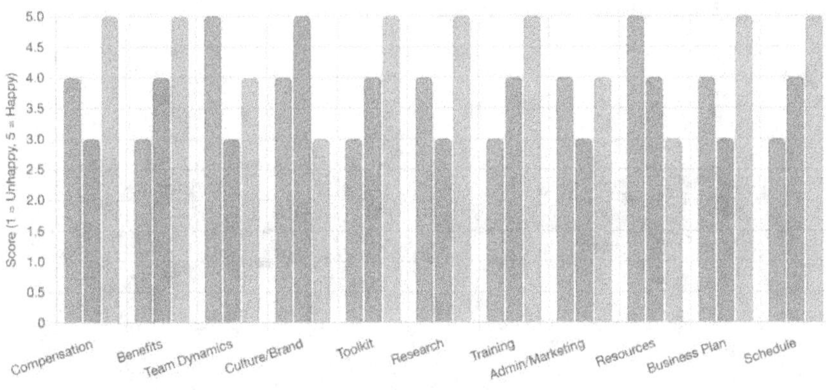

Job Offer Evaluation Across Firms
Score (1 = Unhappy, 5 = Happy)
5.0
4.5
4.0
3.5
3.0
2.5
2.0
1.5
1.0
0.5
0
Compensation
Benefits
Team Dynamics
Culture/Brand
Toolkit
Research
Training
Admin/Marketing
Resources
Business Plan
Schedule
Evaluation Criteria
Firm A
Firm B
Firm C

My First Cold Call

One Saturday morning, I was driving around Athens, Georgia. I was behind the wheel of my trusty hand-me-down 1984 Pontiac Bonneville. My mind wandered, thinking about my plans for...a wedding engagement.

Karen was the girl of my dreams; smart, breathtakingly beautiful, and she laughed at my jokes. Really, the perfect combination. She was the smartest woman I had ever met, except that she would hopefully marry me.

The question of "how" occupied my thoughts for days. As you can imagine, I wanted it to be special and memorable, but also not a copycat kind of approach. And in the dark days before YouTube, Twitter, and Facebook, ideas were a lot harder to come by.

Athens is home to the University of Georgia and the Bulldogs. Karen and I were both in the Redcoat Band; she in the flag line, and I was a brass player. We loved everything about the Redcoats and Georgia Football.

Football in the south is nearly a religion, and the spiritual leader is the head coach. In those days, the great Vince Dooley had the helm. He now has the field at the stadium named after him.

My Bonneville happened to take me by Coach Dooley's house (everyone in town knew where he lived). I slowed a little to look up the hill at the Coach's impressive-looking estate. Then a flash popped into my mind with searing clarity: What if I could ask Karen the big question on the 50-yard line of the UGA football stadium? THAT would be the ticket!

I kept driving past the Dooleys' house and soon pulled into the parking lot of a nearby strip mall. My mind raced with thoughts about Karen. My breathing started to get elevated, and my palms a little moist as I realized what I must do. I had to knock on Coach Vince Dooley's door and ask for his help.

I was going to make my first cold call.

Vince Dooley was a man I had never met in person, and to say that he was a hero in the State of Georgia is an understatement. I might as well be knocking on the front door of the White House. The stakes were huge, and I had no backup plan.

I summoned all the courage I could muster and put the car in gear. I pointed the Bonneville back towards the Dooley estate and soon pulled into the driveway and walked up to the door. My heart was beating quickly as I rang the doorbell.

Coach Dooley's wife, Barbara, answered. She was famous too and almost as widely known as the Coach. She looked at me with some suspicion; a lanky college kid likely up to no good. "Can I help you?" she said. "Ma'am, can I please speak with the Coach?" I muttered. She paused, and after a moment of evaluating the situation, opened the door. "Come on in," she said skeptically.

Just like that, I was walking down the hall of Coach Dooley's home. From idea to reality in 15 minutes.

I remember every detail of the walk in the house. The walls were lined with pictures of the Dooleys with all manner of major celebrities. The walls were half-beadboard, and the floors, hardwood. Finally, we reached the den where the great man was sitting. Coach Dooley was wearing Khaki pants and a white T-shirt and sitting in an easy chair. He was, of course, watching a ball game with reading glasses on his forehead.

After a short intro from his wife, the Coach looked at me and said, "Son, how can I help you?" I managed to spit out, "Coach, can I borrow the stadium?"

He looked a little puzzled, made a funny face, and said, "You're gonna have to tell me a little more than that." I smiled—a slightly embarrassed, nervous smile—and told him about Karen. We were both in the Redcoat Band, I explained. I am second-generation UGA and have attended football games since I was 3 years old. We love the university, and I love her...one big Bulldog love milkshake.

"So, let me get this straight: you want to use the *football stadium* to get engaged?"

"Uh, yes, sir," I said. "Well, that's a first," said the Coach. He went on to say, rubbing his chin. Finally, he looked me right in the eyes and said, "You can't do it during a game, of course, but I'll allow it when the venue is empty." I beamed.

He wrote down a number and said, "Call Tony on Monday, and he will get things set up." I wanted to hug the man. He was very friendly and sympathetic, but ready to get back to his Saturday. I thanked him profusely and retreated.

A Marriage Made In Between The Hedges

Tony was on top of it, and soon we had a plan. I would take Karen to dinner the following week, on Sunday, May 12th, 1991. The University Police were tasked with unlocking the normally highly secured stadium. They would not only leave the gate "false locked" but turn off the fabled laser field alarms.

I met Karen for dinner at DePalmas Italian Cafe—it is still in business! Karen later said she could tell something was up because I didn't finish my meal.

After dinner, I suggested a stroll through campus on a beautiful spring evening. We talked about how we met and how our relationship had grown. We talked about our hopes and our dreams. My stomach churned as we got closer to the hallowed hall of UGA football.

Finally, we made it to the stadium. I tried the gate and, well, it opened! Karen was horrified. My second major sales job was to convince my law-abiding girlfriend to break the law. Finally, after some cajoling, we walked in. The stadium was grand and magical at night. The stillness of the evening was a counterbalance to my beating heart.

As we reached the field and those supposed alarms, I had to convince her again that we were OK. I grabbed both her hands and looked right into her eyes. "Do you trust me?" I said. She slowly nodded yes, and we stepped onto the field.

I'll remember the next two minutes for the rest of my life. We strolled down the field, and I wanted to clap my heels like a happy Irishman. As we approached the 50-yard line, I spotted the goods. A single red rose with an engagement ring on it. The person who was to be my best man was part of the advance team that set up the venue ahead of our arrival.

"Well, what is this?" I asked Karen. She spotted the items and quickly processed the situation. A tear formed in her eye. I knelt on one knee and asked for her hand in marriage.

"YES!" she said, and the deal was sealed. My world was rocked, and I felt at the same time great relief and tremendous excitement.

And then we heard a ROAR. A number of our friends who were previously snuck in and hidden in the upper deck of the stadium jumped up like cheerleaders after a big play. I felt like spiking the ball and yelling, "Touchdown!"

Now, four wonderful kids and nearly 28 years later, I think of these special few days with warm remembrance. Life has been kind to Karen and me, and all these years later, we still love each other very much. We've lived a wonderful life together and have some quarters yet to go.

But I'm also reminded that taking measured risks, social and otherwise, can pay big dividends. Forcing yourself to deal with stretching your comfort zone can open new doors in life. Crossing the threshold of the Dooley household was temporarily discomforting but ultimately life-changing in multiple ways.

Sometimes young people in my business ask, "Does cold calling still work?"

My friends, a wonderful marriage, four kids, and two pugs are all living proof that the answer is YES!

SECTION THREE

On Succeeding

CHAPTER 10

Setting Your Success Strategy

Before we conclude this book, I want to set you up for success. This chapter and the next serve as a primer on some of the key steps I believe you need to take to achieve success in commercial real estate brokerage.

One thought for you at the top. I've been in CRE and major account sales for over 30 years. Sales success is all about action and going in through the "front door." By this, I mean picking up the phone, knocking on the door, or otherwise connecting with a decision maker.

I've seen people try hard to go in through the side door, by which I mean trying to create approaches other than direct outreach. For example, email campaigns, AI bots, and even producing video content to try to attract decision makers to call you. I do all these things, but I consider them the icing on the cake of hardcore business development and sales.

Let me offer another analogy to help weigh in on this issue: football. In a football offense, most of the plays are boring and direct: run left, run right, toss the ball. They are also hard and often fail to advance. The key to success comes from practice, or what I call being brilliant on the basics, like blocking and tackling.

Rarely, a coach will use a trick play to get ahead in the game. The risks are big, as there can certainly be a loss of yards or even a fumble. Occasionally, trick plays work and then make the highlight reels.

I understand how hard it is to directly contact someone via a phone call (call reluctance) or even a text. However, I assure you that boring reach-outs, done with intense focus and strong follow-up, DO work.

Save the trick plays for those special occasions and grind, grind, grind.

Setting Your Marketplace

You face a big decision at the start. Deciding where to focus your efforts and become a true market expert is important. You are going to invest time and energy, so being thoughtful about the choice makes sense. I previously wrote about some different approaches as a tenant rep. I'm going to repeat some of the ideas here for you now.

I do want to put your mind at ease, however. If you choose a submarket or product type that doesn't work for you, you can change it. I did. I was initially assigned as an industrial broker, and with the mentorship of a senior producer in my shop, I switched to the office as a product type. The good news about the change is that today I do both! I developed a deep knowledge of both product types, and this skill set has served me well to this very day.

There are five typical ways to select a CRE marketplace:

1. Submarket/area
2. Radius
3. Product type
4. Vertical
5. Occupier or asset size

Submarket/Area

Real estate has long been recognized as a location-critical asset class. Selecting a city or, in a larger community, a specific area (a submarket) to focus on can yield significant benefits.

First, you have a defined market to learn. You can learn everything about a curated area if you have the time, energy, and the right mindset to focus.

I've had the experience of riding with many local market experts, "field brokers." It is a joy to watch someone with an enormous knowledge point at building after building, and tell the passengers in the car everything about the asset. Knowing that your local broker has that expertise gives you enormous confidence in them. These brokers employ a technique called "farming," in which they select an area and, in addition to having extensive market knowledge, get to know community leaders. They go to the local Lions Club or Chamber meetings and lean in. Often, knowing the city and its elected officials is helpful. Sometimes they sponsor kids' baseball teams. They get KNOWN for being the man or woman in a defined area.

What should you know about real estate in a submarket? Here is a partial list to get you started:

- Name/address of every asset
- Ownership
- Debt and or capital stack, if possible*
- Details of the building, like size, parking ratio, floor plates, and specialized amenities
- Tenants in the building

There are databases of information that can help with capital stacks. A senior broker or research department can help here.

Another dynamic? Who are your competitors in the area, and what are the TIMs (tenants in the market)? Which landlords are making good deals, and which landlords are in trouble? What are the economics of the deals that are being made (also known as "comps" or comparable transactions)?

Radius

Sometimes you can choose a submarket area to canvas, and other times you can select an even smaller area to focus on. Think New York City, with its incredibly dense office market.

The concept of a radius focuses on a very limited area, typically a few blocks or a suburban location within half a mile of an asset. The same principle can apply to industrial settings, but you may need to widen your radius a bit.

What is the center of the radius? It's usually a place where you have recently completed a transaction or have several deals under your belt. If you are new to the business, no problem! Ask your senior or office leader to help select the center of the radius based on where your firm or team has been most recently active.

Why does the radius method work? Focus is important, and deep expertise in any area sells. I believe the credibility gained from having done a deal in the same building or a nearby asset is a significant advantage.

When you hire an attorney to help you close a real estate deal, you wouldn't hire a personal injury lawyer. You'd hire a real estate counselor, and the more experienced the better. Even if you are relatively new to an area, the credibility of the radius method is strong.

Product Type

There are so many verticals in commercial real estate. Everything from data centers to golf courses to cemeteries (yes, it's a thing, and someone has to do it). Being *the* office or industrial professional is beneficial. Being *the* big box broker is better. Or maybe you choose Class B industrial (Google it). The key principle here is to develop expertise in an area that helps you build trust with prospects. In the office, you can be the Class A highest quality or the bargain guy focused on Class B and C. You are only limited by your imagination and the amount of your chosen product in your area. It makes no sense to be the big box guy if there are only nine buildings of that type in your marketplace.

A consideration that can help you choose a product type has nothing to do with the sticks and bricks initially. Where are your relationships (or your team's), and what do they do? In my case, I realized I knew more executives who were likely to be office users. My relationship span naturally led me to the office product type.

Another approach is to look around your community and come to grips with the predominant type of real estate. If you live in a manufacturing community, then it will be plants and industrial. If you live in an area full of data centers, bingo!

Vertical

I love the vertical approach because it is relatively easy to master. What is a vertical? A business vertical, also known as a *vertical market* or *market segment*, is a specific industry or market that focuses on a particular niche. For example: Engineering firms, law firms, accounting firms, and technology firms.

How do you get up to speed so quickly, you might ask? Start with AI and use good prompts with your favorite technology. "Answer as if I am a long-time industry professional and tell me the key issues that leaders in the accounting field are worried about." You can get the goods in about two seconds.

Other places to find knowledge in verticals include trade organizations, trade magazines/shows, college professors who teach in those areas (they love free lunches), and talking to executives in those areas. You can know more about accounting than 99% of Americans in a matter of weeks if you put your head to it.

How does this help you develop business, you might ask? It helps you play the credibility game. When you consult with someone in law, for example, you ask if they are seeing trends 1, 2, or 3 and how these trends impact their business. You can work with your senior broker to "crosswalk" these issues over to real estate. With that plan in hand, you've got something to say. And a reason for someone to meet you for lunch.

Another approach I like is creating a competitive report. Go to "Book of Lists" or equivalent for your area and pull every major firm in your vertical. Then look them up in your company's real estate database. How much space do they take, and can you infer a rental rate? Then, estimate the number of employees they have (LinkedIn is a great source of truth for this). The result? A list of every firm with all the data, AND an assumption of how much they are paying per employee in real estate costs.

Call the managing partners of all the firms and say something like, "I suspect real estate is your second biggest cost after personnel. Would you like to know what all your competitors are paying on a per-person basis?"

Prospect: "Why, yes, I would. When can you stop by?"

Occupier or Asset Class

By "Occupier," we mean the size of the tenant. By "Asset Class," we mean the size of the building(s) in your area.

Let me tell you a story about niches. I have a good friend, let's call him Bruce, who makes a very nice living calling on 5,000-square-foot office tenants from his basement. He has done so for over 20 years and has his own shop. He drives the car, belongs to the club, and has all the trappings of success. He calls himself the "short order cook" of real estate in his area, meaning he does a lot of deals. But boy, does Bruce make the money.

Bruce's plan is brilliant for a few reasons. First, users of 5,000 square feet are not typically approached by people with experience. Senior brokers want bigger deals. But Bruce IS a senior broker, and he can talk the talk. He can talk about the market like a pro and list an enormous number of companies he's represented in an area. Bruce found an area of focus and, through hard work, has become a huge success.

You can focus on the size of the occupier or the size of the building and develop subject matter expertise. Then let the market see you shine. You will have "game" because of your focus.

You need to surround yourself with senior brokers. Get in the office and ask if you can just listen to them talk. You can learn a ton by shadowing senior folks. However, this does require you to ask. Most senior brokers are way too busy to simply offer this up.

Crafting Your Personal Brand for the Marketplace

Once you've identified your prospects in commercial real estate business development, there are two essential components to focus on: selling and building a strong market presence.

Selling is all about speaking and listening with the intent to persuade. If you're reading this, chances are you've already had some experience in sales.

Equally important is establishing your presence in the market. In other words, what do people think about you before you walk into the room? That perception—your brand and influence—is shaped by how consistently and clearly you show up.

With a background in marketing, I think deeply about this. The starting point for building a personal brand is understanding your audience. In marketing, we call this your "avatar," a representation of your ideal client. From there, your job is to uncover what that person fears, struggles with, or hopes to achieve. You can achieve this by speaking with seasoned brokers or engaging in direct conversations with clients and prospects.

Let's try an example. For an office tenant rep, the avatar could be a company CEO. Let's call her Lucy. Lucy is 48 and is a type "A" person, used to accomplishing all her goals. She is smart about money, too, and knows when to hold 'em and when to fold 'em. Lucy wants to build a strong culture in her services company, which has 8,000 knowledge workers spread across 20 offices around the US. She is concerned about several issues, including leasing the right amount of space (too much is wasteful, and not enough will upset employees), creating a suitable office environment, and securing safe and financially stable landlords.

Back to your marketing plan. Many brokers have spent their careers telling others how great they are. This is not the way to win friends and influence people in the current marketplace. Instead, you are focused on making Lucy the "hero." She accomplishes her goals in part because you are a terrific real estate broker. You are helping her go from where she is today to the end of the success rainbow. To do this, establish the "four corners" of what you will talk about in the business context.

Given Lucy's goals, you might talk about:

- Companies that have leased space (and how they use it)
- How to determine if a prospective landlord is healthy
- Workplace trends and how workplaces can help build culture
- Office market trends in your area (which connotes your expertise)

How and where do you talk about your four corners?

You can choose, but here are some options which I call your "broadcast path":

1. Give speeches at local business clubs. "CRE Success Stories" could be your headline, for example.
2. Write for the local newspaper in your market or submarket area.

3. Teach at local universities or trade organizations where executives spend time.

4. Begin an email newsletter. All executives read email, after all.

5. Start a podcast and ask leaders in your market to share how they have dealt with the four corners issues.

6. Write your own blog and post it on LinkedIn, X, etc.

7. Create your own website and write about the four corners there.

8. Bring them up at lunches, dinners, and social occasions.

After you have chosen your path and executed it for a while, they *will* have a brand image of you. Marketing takes time, however. This is a long-term exercise.

Can your four corners change? Yes, as long as they are congruent with what your avatar is thinking and not too radically different. You wouldn't want to go from a business conversation to discussing world history or poetry, for example.

If you want to learn more about this topic, consider joining the CREi Community (Commercial Real Estate Influencers/Innovators), an online community that discusses it. You can find more at www.creisummit.com.

CHAPTER 11

Setting Your Execution Plan

In this chapter, divided into two parts, we will build your execution plan—the foundation that will guide your daily efforts and long-term success in commercial real estate. We'll start by showing you how to identify and connect with the right clients in your chosen market. From there, we'll guide you through how to create a focused business development plan—a practical approach to consistently winning work. You'll learn how to use technology and data to work not just harder, but smarter. We'll also cover how to build and grow relationships the right way, because people still do business with people they know and trust. Time management is another key area. We'll examine how to apply the 80/20 rule to ensure your time is spent where it matters most. Finally, we'll explore the fundamentals of sales: how to speak clearly, ask great questions, and listen to help your client make the best decision. This is where all the pieces come together, and you start putting your plan into action.

PART A. The Why Before the What

Purpose-Driven Work

Let's begin with the *why* before the *what*. When I got started in commercial real estate, all I could think about was money. My money. I had none, which helped me focus! The reality is, you can't think that way. Your professional success is a direct result of delivering significant value, knowledge, and expertise to your chosen field. Put another way, when you help others succeed, you will too. *How do you help others succeed?* A CFO or real estate director is not looking for "sticks and bricks" because they are cool. They are looking for a physical envelope in which to conduct business. You can help others succeed by understanding their business needs first. Asking a ton of questions up front can really help you as you work to bring real estate solutions to business problems. And not the other way around.

In my career, the biggest win for me is consistently receiving the "atta boy" from a happy client with a smile on their face. I LOVE to see clients get a promotion, a bonus, or a raise when we collectively solve real estate problems. The money on the voucher is nice. But the real motivation is seeing the smile on that CFO's face at the closing dinner!

The Battle Plan: Systems for Business Development

The reality is, you can't help others reach their goals unless they know, trust, and respect you. That's the core of business development. The professionals who can consistently bring in new business, often called "rainmakers," are among the highest earners in our industry. I believe you either are or will become one of them. That's why you're here.

What I want you to understand about the system I'll outline below is this: it's *a* system, not *the* system for success in tenant representation. There are many paths to building a strong business. Some brokers generate deals through relationships at the country club or their kids' Little League games. If that's working for you, keep going.

Others leverage digital tools, artificial intelligence, and large language models to find creative ways to connect with decision-makers and win business. That's a valid path too; keep going there as well.

What defines a *system*, though, is structure. It's a consistent, disciplined approach carried out over time. Just like football players and musicians need to practice, brokers need to work at their craft. Excellence takes time, repetition, and effort. And truthfully, success often starts with belief. You must believe that you can—and will—succeed. At first, progress may be slow. But over time, it builds. And then it accelerates.

Ultimately, I hope you'll take this collection of ideas and, with the help of a senior broker, coach, or mentor, shape it into *your* system—one that works for you. And don't be surprised if your system evolves as your confidence and success grow in this field.

How to Find Clients in Your Chosen Market

Finding the right clients in commercial real estate starts with understanding them deeply. It's more than collecting contact information; it's about understanding their needs, goals, and challenges.

Understand Client Needs First

Begin with a thorough needs assessment. Ask strategic questions to understand:

- Their business model and growth plans
- Operational and space requirements
- Budget constraints
- Preferred locations
- Challenges they face now or anticipate facing soon

The goal is alignment. The better you understand the situation, the better you can position yourself to help them.

Define Your Focus, Then Build Your Strategy

Once you've chosen your area of focus—say, representing Class A office tenants in a 30-million-square-foot submarket—it's time to build your client discovery strategy.

Think like a college football coach preparing for a major game. Coaches study film, analyze opponents, and plan relentlessly. You should, too.

Here's a five-part approach to building your strategy:

1. Learn the Market: Start by identifying the major buildings in your submarket. If you're a visual learner, visit them in person. Seeing the buildings helps you retain information better than just reviewing databases.

Create a simple "building check sheet" for each asset, capturing key data such as:

- Total rentable square footage
- Number of floors and floor plate size
- Parking ratio (e.g., 4 spaces per 1,000 SF)
- Building ownership and leasing agents
- Debt profile (capital stack)*
- Key tenants
- Amenities (e.g., gyms, cafés)
- Asking rents and comps
- Broker entry points

Ask a senior broker to help you access debt information. TREPP is a great resource for public debt data.

Pro tip: Tour buildings on Saturday mornings. They're open, traffic is lighter, and it's a great time to explore. Later, have a colleague quiz you to build fluency.

2. Connect with VIPs: Early in my career, a senior tenant rep advised me to make a list of 50 VIPs I wanted to meet.

When I asked who qualified as a VIP, he said:

"Political leaders, newspaper editors, landlords, business leaders, and nonprofit heads—anyone with influence in your market."

The purpose? To gain insight into the strengths, weaknesses, opportunities, and threats (SWOT) in your submarket.

I met with transportation officials, editors, leasing agents, chamber leaders, and economic development directors. Many are still in my network decades later.

How to reach out:

- Research them beforehand (social media, news, LinkedIn)
- Call them, not email, to request a meeting
- Introduce yourself and mention something you admire about their work
- Ask for a short coffee meeting to hear about their path and get their view on the market

Asking for advice is powerful. It shows humility and curiosity, qualities people respect.

After the meeting:

- Log their info in your CRM
- Track follow-ups and key takeaways
- Stay in touch via birthdays, holiday greetings, and market updates

3. Identify and Study Competitors: Understanding your competitors is critical. Not to badmouth them, but to learn from them and differentiate yourself.

Ask:

- Who are the key brokers doing deals in your submarket?
- What kinds of clients do they work with?
- How do they present their value proposition?

Search their names online, review their websites, and study their LinkedIn profiles. Many brokers openly share client wins and strategies. You'll learn what works, and what gaps you can fill.

Talk to landlord brokers and senior advisors. They'll know who's active. VIPs from earlier meetings can also tell you who's making moves.

Important: Never engage in "negative selling." It makes you look unprofessional. Focus on your strengths and let others worry about theirs.

4. Learn the Major Tenants: If you're representing office tenants, you need to know who they are.

Many brokerages offer databases to help you find tenants, their lease expiration dates, and basic company information. Target tenants whose leases expire within the next three to five years.

Log key details in your CRM, including:

- Industry and size
- Key leaders and contacts
- Personal or professional connections you may have
- Business challenges real estate could help solve (e.g., hybrid work, parking shortages, talent attraction)

To discover more:

- Read public companies' 10-K reports (esp. the Management's Discussion and Section 2B)
- Review earnings calls for strategic priorities
- Check Glassdoor, Reddit, or LinkedIn for employee feedback
- Use LinkedIn Navigator to track hiring, attrition, and company growth
- Search for trade group white papers or articles about the firm

- Talk to their landlord or the local chamber for additional intel

Start with macro questions (e.g., "How's business going?"), and then drill into specifics ("Are they struggling with retention or space utilization?").

5. Identify Leadership and Find Problems You Can Solve

Think of yourself as a business detective. You're not just learning *about* a company, you're looking for "purchase points" that could open the door to a conversation with decision-makers.

This skill takes time to develop but pays huge dividends.

Consider Harvey Mackay's famous strategy. He started out selling envelopes—an undifferentiated product—and built his company by learning more about his customers than anyone else.

His salespeople used a tool called *Mackay 66* to gather deep personal and professional details about clients. You don't need to replicate it exactly, but the takeaway is clear:

> **People care less about how much you know and more about how much you know about *them*.**

That's how trust is built—and trust drives deals.

Final Thoughts

Client discovery is not a one-time task; it is an ongoing process. It's an ongoing discipline that separates average reps from great ones. Use this approach as a foundation, then tailor it to your specific needs with the guidance of your coach or senior advisor.

Over time, as you build relationships, gather insights, and refine your outreach, you'll create a system that's effective and entirely your own.

PART B. The Battle Plan for Success

Create a Business Development Plan: Battle Plan for Success

I was fortunate to spend time with the legendary John Cushman of Cushman & Wakefield. John was a true giant in business development, having led some of the largest tenant representation deals in history. During our time together, he shared a simple but powerful approach that has stayed with me ever since. He said, "Ken, you gotta find 'em, mind 'em, and grind 'em." I've reflected on those words many times over the years, and they've become a guiding principle in my approach to business development.

"Find 'em" refers to the process of identifying and qualifying prospective clients. We discussed this in depth in Section Two. *"Mind 'em"* means staying top of mind—consistently nurturing relationships with your prospects through relevant, thoughtful outreach. *"Grind 'em"* comes into play when you get invited to pitch or win the business. At that point, you double down with relentless effort to deliver exceptional results and exceed expectations. This simple framework captures the heart of successful tenant rep brokerage.

However, to put this philosophy into practice, you need a structured, repeatable game plan. That's where your Business Development Battle Plan, or BDBP, comes in. Writing your BDBP is a foundational step toward long-term success. It forces you to think critically about your strategy, define your goals, and establish the daily actions required to build your pipeline and client base. It's not just a plan; it's your playbook. It should guide how you spend your time, track your progress, and make adjustments as you learn what works.

Like a gym workout, your BDBP should be personalized. There's no one-size-fits-all solution. Everyone's market, style, and strengths are different.

What follows is one example of a plan, built around phone outreach, because phone calls absolutely work. However, you should adapt the approach to fit your voice, your local market, and the guidance you receive from senior brokers and mentors. Email outreach should also be part of your plan. Executives read email all day, and a well-written message can open doors. In some cases, direct messages through LinkedIn or other platforms can also be effective. Ultimately, the best outreach strategy is the one you'll actually use; one that consistently helps you start meaningful conversations with decision-makers.

The key is to build a plan that fits you, and then execute it with discipline. We'll walk you through a step-by-step method to build your battle plan. You'll learn how to create a call capacity schedule, track your progress with a point system, and set yourself up for long-term success in tenant rep business development.[4]

Business Development Plan for New Brokers

This plan serves as your guide to building and managing a "basket" of 400 prospects to help you grow your client base as a new broker. It's designed to be clear, actionable, and motivating, with a focus on urgency, accountability, and handling rejection confidently. Think of it as your roadmap to turning prospects into clients while staying organized and motivated.

Step 1: Build Your Prospect Basket

Your goal is to create a basket of 400 prospects, categorized into three levels based on their likelihood to need your services. Don't try to find all 400 at once; this is about starting small and acting fast.

---

[4] Link to tables (Call Capacity and Points System) https://docs.google.com/spreadsheets/d/1huSdUqy0UDKMaE66AbPBnYR-d6OKfq1vj34Iqo6_tVw/edit?usp=sharing

Here's how to categorize and manage them:

Prospect Levels

1. **A-Level Prospects** (High Priority)
    - **Definition**: Companies with a high chance of needing your services within the next **30 days** (e.g., expiring leases, known expansion needs).
    - **Goal**: Urgently secure a meeting with a decision-maker ASAP.
    - **Action**: Call, email, or visit to set up a meeting within 1-2 weeks. Be persistent but professional.
    - **Mindset**: Treat A-listers like they're "lucky" to be on your radar.

2. **B-Level Prospects** (Medium Priority)
    - **Definition**: Companies likely to need services within the next 12-14 months.
    - **Goal**: Build familiarity and credibility so they think of you when they're ready. Monitor for changes (e.g., expansion plans) that could bump them to A-level.
    - **Action**: Make initial contact (call or email) to introduce yourself. Follow up every 3-6 months to stay on their radar.
    - **Mindset**: Look for opportunities to "promote" them to A-level if new information suggests urgency.

3. **C-Level Prospects** (Low Priority)
    - **Definition**: Companies with long-term leases or no immediate need, but worth keeping an eye on.
    - **Goal**: Establish basic awareness so they know who you are "just in case."
    - **Action**: Send an introductory email or connect via LinkedIn. Check in semi-annually to maintain contact.

- **Mindset**: These are your long-term bets. Stay professional, but don't invest too much time.

Tips for Building the Basket

- **Start Small**: Don't try to find all 400 prospects at once (no "boiling the ocean"). Begin with 10-20 companies in your submarket and expand weekly.
- **Sources**: Use LinkedIn, local business directories, or your brokerage's CRM to identify companies. Look for lease data or news about expansions.
- **Action Timeline**: Spend 1-2 weeks initially identifying 50 prospects (10 A-level, 20 B-level, 20 C-level). Add 10-20 prospects weekly until you reach 400.
- **Measurable Outcome**: By the end of month one, have 100 prospects categorized (20 A, 40 B, 40 C). By month three, aim for the full 400.

Step 2: Create a Points-Based Accountability System

Think of this system as "gutter guards" in bowling: it keeps you on track and ensures you use your time effectively. Be honest about your efforts; fudging the numbers only hurts your progress.

How It Works

- Assign points to daily prospecting activities to measure your effort.
- Example point system:
  - Make a cold call: **2 points**
  - Send a personalized email: **1 point**
  - Secure a meeting with an A-level prospect: **10 points**
  - Follow up with a B-level prospect: **3 points**

o   Connect with a C-level prospect (e.g., LinkedIn): **1 point**

o   Research a prospect (max 15 minutes): **1 point**

- **Daily Goal**: Aim for **20 points per day** (e.g., 5 calls, 5 emails, 5 research tasks).
- **Weekly Goal**: Achieve **100 points per week** and review your progress every Friday.

Tools

- Use your brokerage's CRM (e.g., Salesforce) or a simple spreadsheet to track points and activities.
- Log calls, emails, and outcomes (e.g., Left voicemail, Scheduled meeting).
- **Measurable Outcome**: By week 4, consistently hit 100 points per week and have at least 2 A-level meetings scheduled.

Step 3: Set Up Your Call Environment

Having a consistent setup helps you stay focused and professional during prospecting.

Workspace Checklist

- **Location**: Choose a quiet spot (an office, a home desk, or a coffee shop with good Wi-Fi).
- **Gear**: Phone, laptop, CRM access, notepad or tablet for notes, headset for clear calls.
- **Beverage**: Grab coffee, water, or your drink of choice to stay energized.
- **Mindset Prep**: Remind yourself:
  1. "I have the best job in the world. Making calls and closing deals beats working in a salt mine!"

2. "My services are valuable, and these companies are lucky to work with me."

Call Schedule

- Dedicate **2 hours daily** (e.g., 9:00-11:00 a.m.) for calls and emails.
- Block off time for research (30 minutes daily) and follow-ups (30 minutes daily).
- **Measurable Outcome**: Make 10 calls and send 5 emails daily, logging all interactions in your CRM or spreadsheet.

Step 4: Clear Roadmap with Timelines and Outcomes

Here's a three-month roadmap to build your basket, make progress, and start closing deals:

Month 1: Build and Start

- **Week 1-2**: Identify 50 prospects (10 A, 20 B, 20 C). Make initial calls/emails to 20 prospects. Goal: 1 A-level meeting scheduled.
- **Week 3-4**: Add 50 more prospects (total 100). Hit 100 points weekly. Goal: 2 A-level meetings scheduled, 10 B-level follow-ups completed.
- **Outcome**: 100 prospects categorized, 20 points daily, 2-3 A-level meetings booked.

Month 2: Expand and Engage

- **Week 5-8**: Add 150 prospects (total 250). Make 10 calls/day, focusing on A-level prospects. Schedule site tours for A-level prospects who show interest.
- **Key Actions**:
  - **Site Tours**: Offer A-level prospects a tour of potential properties (aim for 1-2 tours by week 8).

- ○ **Follow-Ups**: Check in with B-level prospects every 3 months, and with C-level prospects annually.
- **Outcome**: 250 prospects, 4-5 A-level meetings, 1-2 site tours completed.

Month 3: Scale and Negotiate

- **Week 9-12**: Reach 400 prospects. Focus on converting A-level meetings into negotiations.
- **Key Actions**:
  - ○ **Negotiation Stages**: For A-level prospects, move from meetings to proposals (Weeks 9-10) to signed deals (Weeks 11-12).
  - ○ **Monitor B-Level**: Research B-level prospects for changes (e.g., news about expansions) to promote to A-level.
- **Outcome**: 400 prospects, 6-8 A-level meetings, 2-3 proposals sent, 1 deal closed.

Step 5: Handling Rejection: "Pushing for the No"

Rejection is part of prospecting, but it's not personal. The "pushing for the no" strategy helps you stay confident and move on quickly.

- **What It Means**: Instead of fearing rejection, aim to get a clear "yes" or "no" from prospects. A "no" frees you to focus on better opportunities.
- **How to Do It**:
  - ○ Be direct: "Is now a good time to discuss your upcoming lease needs, or should we reconnect later?"
  - ○ If they hesitate, push gently: "I want to respect your time. If this isn't a priority now, can I check back in three months?"
  - ○ Accept "no" gracefully: "Thanks for letting me know! I'll keep you in mind for future opportunities."

- **Mindset**: A "no" is a win. It clarifies who to prioritize and saves time. Celebrate moving on to better prospects.
- **Measurable Outcome**: By month 2, aim for 5 "Nos" per week from A-level prospects to refine your list and focus on high-potential leads.

Final Notes

- **Stay Honest**: Track your points and calls accurately. Lying about your efforts only slows your progress, like cheating at the gym.
- **Stay Positive**: You're offering a valuable service, and every call brings you closer to a deal.
- **Act Fast**: Don't over-research. Start calling within the first week. Time is ticking!

By following this plan, you'll build a robust prospect basket, stay accountable, and turn rejections into opportunities. You've got this. Go make those calls and close some deals!

CHAPTER 12

Leverage Technology and Data: Work Smarter *and* Harder

This section is somewhat of a moving target, as technology evolves rapidly; however, there are still some enduring principles worth sharing when it comes to building a robust "tech stack."

I like to think of a tenant rep as similar to a carpenter. A carpenter has different tools for different jobs—a hammer, a saw, and a level. The tools themselves may change over time, but their purpose stays largely the same. In tenant representation, your tools serve specific functions, and the more skilled you are with them, the better your results will be.

First, you need tools to support relationship management. A solid customer relationship management (CRM) system enables you to track clients and prospects, manage follow-ups, and keep a pulse on your pipeline. It's the foundation of your outreach strategy.

Next, deal management platforms are important. These platforms help you organize transaction documents, track progress, and collaborate with clients and team members. Think of them as a specialized form of project management software, designed for real estate transactions.

Financial analysis and modeling software is also a must. These tools allow you to create executive-level dashboards and clearly present side-by-side comparisons of leasing or ownership options, helping your clients make informed decisions. Related to that are budgeting tools, which are especially helpful when working with project managers. They allow you to calculate and communicate the total cost of leasing or owning space over time, something clients value deeply.

GIS and mapping tools are incredibly useful for visualizing market data and comparing potential locations. They help clients see spatial patterns and scenarios that influence their choices. Workflow automation tools, such as email responders or appointment schedulers, free up your time from low-value tasks, allowing you to focus on what drives results.

Collaboration and scheduling platforms such as video conferencing apps, calendar syncing, and shared workspaces are essential in this era of remote communication. They're closely tied to workflow automation but serve a broader purpose in team and client engagement. Similarly, cloud-based document management is now a baseline expectation. If you're still keeping paper files on your desk, it's time to evolve.

eSignature and digital contract tools help accelerate the deal process. The era of wet signatures is coming to an end; digital execution is faster, cleaner, and is now expected by most clients today.

On the intelligence side, business insight platforms can be game-changers. They allow you to research companies in depth before you ever speak to them. With the right tools, you can access contact information, executive profiles, and company history, giving you the confidence and insight to walk into a meeting.

Social media, especially professional platforms, can't be overlooked. People freely share their career paths, current roles, and even interests. This self-reported information is incredibly valuable for building rapport before a meeting or call.

Now, you may be wondering why I haven't recommended specific tools by name. The answer is simple: the tech landscape changes too rapidly.

More importantly, I want you to take the initiative. Ask your senior brokers, colleagues, and mentors what they use and why. Your tech stack should be built not just on the latest apps, but on tools that work in your market and workflow.

The bottom line is this: a well-chosen, thoughtfully assembled tech stack helps you move faster, make smarter decisions, and ultimately serve your clients better. But like any craftsman, you must know your tools inside and out. Master the ones that matter most to your business, sharpen that digital saw, and you'll be unstoppable.

Time Management and the 2080 Principle: Protecting Your Non-Renewable Resource

One of the trade-offs of being a commercial real estate broker is that it can be challenging to determine the value of your time. If you were paid a salary, the math is pretty simple. But how do you determine where and how to allocate your time?

To help young brokers understand the value of their time, I devised a simple exercise. Let's begin.

There are 2,080 working hours in a year: $52 \times 40 = 2,080$ (you can factor in vacation separately). To find your hourly rate, divide the compensation you'd like to make by the number of working hours in a year. For example, if your goal is to gross $1,000,000 per year (including paying your broker 50%), then $1,000,000 \div 2,080 = \$481$ per hour.

If you have the noble goal of earning $1 million a year, then let's double the $481 an hour and round up, so your time is worth $1,000 an hour in that scenario.

In practice, this approach allows you to put boundaries on your time. If you've taken a kid bowling, the facility can turn on "gutter guards" that keep the ball from rolling into the gutter. I think about time management in the same way, guards to keep you focused on what is in front of you.

Let's look at some examples.

You get a call from a landlord in a submarket 30 miles from your office. You only occasionally do work there. The friendly landlord is inviting you to a "broker party" to see their asset. They are offering free lunch (pork sandwiches) and a chance to win a flat-screen TV in a draw.

It will take you one hour round-trip to get there, and you will spend an hour at the event. So, using our math above, if your time is worth $1,000 an hour, then you just "spent" $2,000 to get a "free" pork sandwich, a building tour, and a chance to win a TV.

Are there times when you should attend an event like this? Sure! Some reasons I would go:

- I'm doing a deal with the landlord
- The event features a new or remodeled asset that I've not yet toured
- A landlord calls and asks me to come by as a favor (favors work both ways)
- I have a tenant prospect with whom I'd like to share more about the asset

Another lens I use is dividing activities into two groups: high-payback and low-payback.

Examples of high payback activities for me:

- Giving a speech in my community
- Taking a prospect to lunch or dinner
- Appearing on a business podcast that business leaders listen to

- Calling or otherwise connecting with large tenants who have leases expiring in the next two to five years
- Reviewing a lease on a deal I am working on
- Conducting a property tour
- Talking with a landlord and updating on market conditions

Examples of low payback activities for me:

- Completing expense reports
- Many meetings
- Completing a financial analysis (I have analysts for this purpose)
- Chasing unqualified leads
- Taking coffee meetings with people who want to "pick my brain" but cannot offer business opportunities

How you use your time will change as you advance in the business. At the beginning of your career, you essentially trade your time for money. Your day may be filled with many low-payback activities (think administrative tasks) that other, more senior folks ask you to do.

However, as your career advances, you can focus more and more on high-payback activities and delegate low-payback tasks to others. When you focus on high-payback activities such as conversations with important clients and high-level business development, then you are trading your *value* for money. This is the goal, and it will allow you to generate better income AND a better work/life balance!

Mastering Sales: Speaking and Listening with the Intent to Convince

Many people mistakenly believe that sales is "yucky" or demeaning, a last-resort career path, or something to avoid. In reality, sales is a noble and essential calling. In virtually every industry, the people who can consistently bring in new business—those who can "make it rain"—are often the highest compensated and most valued contributors.

Sales is not limited to traditional roles. It also plays a central part in leadership. A CEO is constantly selling ideas to their board, just as a board chair must win the confidence of investors. At its core, sales involves persuasion, influence, and trust, all skills that are vital in high-stakes decision-making and leadership.

There are countless great books on the subject (see Appendix 4), but based on over 25 years of experience in major account sales, I've found four principles to be especially important.

First, **sales is about discovery**. Your ability to ask insightful questions, listen well, and remember the answers will set you apart from the competition. Leading with curiosity and empathy builds credibility and opens doors. Listen first, talk second. One excellent resource on this is *Questions That Sell* by Paul Cherry, which emphasizes the power of the right questions.

Second, you must **understand what motivates your client** to change or take action. What pain points are they trying to fix? What aspirations are they trying to reach? When you understand what drives someone, you can tailor your solutions to their personal or professional goals. This approach solves problems and builds trust. For a deeper dive into this topic, I recommend *Drive: The Surprising Truth About What Motivates Us* by Daniel Pink.

Third, **learn to tell compelling stories**. Your ability to articulate how you've helped others solve similar problems can be incredibly persuasive. Keep your storytelling tight; speak succinctly and avoid rambling. The best sales conversations involve the prospect doing most of the talking. Your stories should enhance their trust, not dominate the conversation.

One of the best books on storytelling is *Storyworthy: Engage, Teach, Persuade, and Change Your Life Through the Power of Storytelling* by Matthew Dicks.

Finally, **be easy to talk to and build genuine relationships with**. Being likable doesn't mean being charming or slick; it means taking a sincere interest in the other person's life and remembering what they share with you. These small acts of thoughtfulness compound over time. A great resource on relationship building is Harvey Mackay's *Swim with the Sharks Without Being Eaten Alive*, which offers practical advice on connecting with people meaningfully and memorably.

When you approach sales as an act of service—helping others discover solutions, telling meaningful stories, and building real relationships—it becomes something far more than a job. It becomes a way to lead, influence, and make a lasting impact.

A "Bonus" and a Secret Weapon

Being able to read nonverbal cues is a ninja secret for getting people to like you and do what you would like them to do! You've heard others make statements like "85% of communications occur through nonverbals," correct? Learn how to read others, and you will see your success go through the roof.

One of the very best books on the subject is Joe Navarro's *What Every Body Is Saying*. I've actually met Joe in real life, and I was nervous! I knew he could read everything I was thinking from my non-verbal cues. As it turns out, he is a tremendous and friendly man who is very generous with his time and advice. I've read the book multiple times and can highly recommend it to you!

Your Real Estate Prescription

Before we reach the end and discuss your projected career success, I want to check in on your real estate prescription. Did you take notes and create your personal Real Estate Prescription?

If you did, congratulations, and get going!

If you are "still getting to it," then pull the worksheet out and get started. Write down at least five things you are going to do to advance the ball. Create due dates for accountability. Get after it. The time is now!

Conclusion: Your Career Launch

You made it! You ran the race of getting hired. You are onboarded with your team. You know what success looks like. You have your target list all set up.

What next?

Keep after it. This can be a lonely business, but I know that hustle, smart cold calling, and focus WILL pay off. Maintain the network you built during your job search. Continue to expand and go to lunch with people. This is a "blacksmith" type business in the sense that you can learn from more senior folks. Also, building a friend group of other young real estate professionals can be very helpful. You will have bad days, and it's good to know there are others on the journey with you. Lean in on senior brokers in your office and respectfully hold them accountable for mentorship commitments. Write it all down. Maybe YOU will be the one writing your version of the book you've just read someday. Reviewing your learnings helps them "stick" in your head.

We've likely not met, but I am pulling for you. You've got this!

One more thing. When you are successful, your success blesses others. Your clients win. Your company and senior brokers win. Your family wins. So do many others. You buy a car, a house, and a suit, and those vendors win. When you win, an entire community of people wins because of you.

Burn the boats. Let's get after it and head to win after win!

CHAPTER 13

Success Vignettes

"I find that the harder I work,
the more luck I seem to have." – Thomas Jefferson

I'd like to conclude the book with what I call "success vignettes." These consist of a series of short essays that explain the methods and approaches I've used in my brokerage journey.

I hope they'll be helpful to you as well.

Accountability 101

The Friday 5. Speedy Accountability

Find a friend in another industry with goals to meet. They can be anything from business to personal. Meet and have a meal to discuss those goals in detail. Each of you should write three or four accountability questions that you will ask each other.

Then set a time, perhaps Friday at 9:00 a.m., for a five-minute call. Show up and ask each other the questions, and do not lie. Truth will set you free. You will find that your Thursdays become highly productive!

The Points System

Sales is hard in part because you go home at the end of the day, not sure what you've accomplished. I know how to fix that issue: a points system.

Identify the tasks that will help you be successful. A phone call, leaving a voicemail, having a phone conversation with a prospect and "talking business," having a sales call, leading a pitch, and then getting hired are all on my list. Assign a point value to each task, and then set weekly and monthly point goals.

ACTIVITY	POINT VALUE
A sales phone call	1
Leaving a voicemail	2
Having a phone conversation with a prospect and 'talking business'	10
Having a sales call in person or by video (presenting credentials)	25
Leading or participating in a formal sales pitch	50
Getting hired	75

If your goal is to achieve 150 points a week, then getting hired is the best way! I say that a little tongue-in-cheek, but the system allows you to govern your behavior and know how close you are to achieving your goal.

A word about cheating. I know you would never cheat and take credit for an activity that did not really occur. But if you do, you'll only be hurting yourself. The analogy is going to the gym and not giving your workout your all. You are just wasting time!

Now, what are you waiting for? Get after it!

The Pareto Principle: Doing More with Less

Vilfredo Pareto, an Italian economist and sociologist, is best known for his contributions to economic theory and sociology, particularly through the development of the Pareto Principle. Born on July 15, 1848, in Paris, Pareto's work has had a lasting impact on various fields, including economics and business management.

Pareto initially studied engineering at the Polytechnic University of Turin, where he earned a degree in civil engineering in 1870. This technical background provided Pareto with a strong foundation in mathematics and analytical thinking, which he later applied to his work in economics and sociology.

Pareto's most significant contribution to economics is the Pareto Principle, also known as the 80/20 rule. This principle emerged from his observation that roughly 80% of the land in Italy was owned by 20% of the population.

His most important observation is used by high-producing business leaders today. He extended the 80/20 principle, suggesting that in many systems, 80% of the effects come from 20% of the causes. In other words, not every effort yields an equal return.

80% of your success can be traced to only 20% of the things you do in a week.

How can you put this to work in real estate brokerage? Sit down with your team leader or a mentor and identify the most important things you are doing to contribute to the team's success. For example, if your contribution involves setting meetings, try to determine what makes you most successful in getting decision-makers to meet. Then try and do MORE of whatever that is. I call the things you do exceptionally well your genius. Identify your genius and do more of it.

Here is one more way to illustrate the Pareto principle. If you think of the musician Billy Joel, he is a genius at performing in front of crowds. He gets paid a lot of money to entertain people. What does Billy Joel not do? He doesn't sell tickets, doesn't make the popcorn or the t-shirts, and he certainly doesn't clean up after the concert. All this is delegated to others.

Figure out why people (including your leadership) will pay you bigger dollars and vigorously try to increase your skill and time spent on those tasks. Vilfredo will be proud of you.

How to Work a Cocktail Party: 8 Steps to Success

Connecting in person is critical to success in the CRE environment. But how do you walk right up to someone of great importance and simply say hello?

Like much of real estate, a cocktail party is a confidence game. Being prepared and intentional can make all the difference in your return on time invested (ROI). Believe me, a cocktail party isn't about the food, the venue, and certainly not the booze. This is a golden opportunity for you to connect with VIP's and advance your brand one handshake at a time.

1. Be Prepared

If possible, call the event organizer and request a guest list, which you can review in advance of the party. Another option is to arrive early and scan the name tag table for folks you might want to speak to during your time. If all else fails, take a deep breath, smile, and stick out your hand.

2. Start Strong

Make a lasting impression and ensure your elevator pitch is ready for that specific audience. Your answer to "What do you do for a living?" is your pitch. How can you turn your statement into a "USP" (a unique selling proposition), given your audience of the moment?

3.   Practice the 75/25 Principle

Everyone is tuned into their own needs, wants, and problems. If you ask a lot of "other-focused" questions (75% focused on them), truly listen and respond thoughtfully, then you will differentiate yourself from most people. Many attend cocktail parties and "talk at" others as opposed to really listening. You honor the other person when you focus and actively listen. (By the way, most people assume you are an expert; they care what you know about them and what you can remember the next time you meet.)

4.   Position Yourself as a Problem Solver and Professional Matchmaker

Making helpful introductions is a tried-and-true way to get more time with a decision maker. Listen carefully for business problems and consider ways to engage. A surefire way to endear yourself to someone is to help their children or grandchildren when they are trying to enter the workforce.

5.   Don't Be a "Shoulder Surfer"

One thing that drives me crazy is when you observe people at parties who are looking over people's shoulders for better name tags. Everyone appreciates respect, and engaging with someone for 90-120 seconds won't kill you. Remember, even people who seemingly can't help you (such as vendors) have their own networks too. High-level politicians understand this concept well. A little focus and patience can come back in amazing ways.

6.   Work Is a Verb

You are at the party to work. I often eat before I go or step aside and grab some food. Often, I eat nothing at the party and just have a social drink.

The food and beverages are beside the point for you. Your entire mission is to make solid connections with several people.

7. The Goal Isn't to Meet Everyone

This isn't your wedding, and you're most likely not the guest of honor. Meeting everyone in the room is usually impossible and could make you seem rude. Plus, you can appear to be "that guy" that no one thinks is sincere. If you walk away with three great new opportunities, then you've won the game.

8. It Ain't Over When It's Over

Ask for their business card first, rather than shoving yours in their face ("May I please have your business card?"). Then you can offer yours in return. After I finish an important interaction, I jot notes on the back and fold the corners of the business cards of important contacts. As soon as I get home or to the office, I jot down or dictate follow-up notes. Many people fail to follow up here, wasting their efforts with little to no results.

Sending VIPs a handwritten note the next morning is a classy move. Follow up with a phone call that references the conversation you had with them. Demonstrate you are an active listener by asking about the business problem, relative, or life situation they shared. Then ask for a meeting to talk more.

Congratulations, you have now taken the time to approach an age-old tradition like a true professional. People will notice your style and grace; you are a winner!

Delegation by Spinning Plates

Delegation is hard. However, most people recognize that delegation is one of the keys to success, and doing more with less of your time will help you win the business game. Delegation helps you manage your time AND your energy. You have to manage both.

Over 30 years in business, I've developed a method I call "spinning plates." I didn't read this approach in a book; I've lived it. It's really simple, and for me, highly effective.

There are just five keys and a "bonus" at the end.

First, I call it "spinning plates" because there are circus performers who have an act in which they spin many plates. Just when you think a rack of plates is going to come crashing down, the performer somehow catches it and spins it up again. They can do this with an amazing number of plates. It's fun and scary at the same time to watch!

Here are my five keys to delegation by spinning plates for more complex projects that require weeks to complete:

1. **Clear direction.** Precisely what are you asking your teammate to do? Think of this like a recipe for baking a cake. What ingredients are needed, in what order, and how do you wish the

cake to be made? Don't miss a step, or you will not have the beautiful pastry you are imagining.

2. **What does winning look like?** Imagine that cake covered with frosting. Now, make sure the vision of exactly what you want is clearly communicated. Examples, including pictures and graphics, are helpful. Most business problems are not original, so find where someone else has solved the problem and highlight that solution.

3. **15 minutes of a spin session per week.** This is the heartbeat of my delegation. Progress communication either in person or via video meeting, NOT email. Your teammate needs to see your smiling face to keep the plate spinning. Or, maybe your frown if things are not advancing. Demonstrate your commitment to this project by being present for 15 minutes.

4. **Detailed note-taking.** You. Must. Capture. Progress. (Or lack thereof) Every week. We all have too much going on. You can refer back to notes to see what happened six weeks ago, and those notes could explain why we are where we are today. I am a big fan of shared documents like Google Docs and Sheets.

5. **If you are delegating a relatively simple task like making a flyer or running a survey, you can think of plate-spinning differently.** Keep notes on the "reps"—the work product—and seek to help your teammate improve it every rep. The goal is for them to become so proficient and independent that you can send them a brief email, and they'll return the perfect product to you. This may take a few tries, but you can do it!

Bonus: The draft email approach. I once heard a CEO share his delegation method. After a meeting with a subordinate, he takes detailed notes and pens a draft email *as if* the project is complete. Then, a few weeks before the deadline, he sends an email with all the meeting details and requests an update on the status. He reported with a big smile that people are stunned by his excellent memory, but he just recorded his thoughts while they were fresh in a draft email!

Good luck on this delegation journey. The ROI is high! Now go spin some plates!

APPENDICES

The Prescription Worksheet

The Prescription: A Personalized Roadmap to CRE Success

The Real Estate Prescription (TREP) is a tool I developed after meeting with hundreds of young people over the years. It is a practical, actionable tool designed to bridge the gap between aspiration and achievement in the commercial real estate (CRE) industry.

Modeled after a medical prescription, it serves as a customized "treatment plan" for individuals, particularly young professionals or career changers, seeking to enter or advance in CRE, with a focus on tenant representation brokerage.

At its core, the Prescription summarizes the "diagnosis" of your professional health, identifying strengths such as strong communication skills or relevant prior experience, while pinpointing areas for improvement, including gaps in market knowledge, networking deficiencies, or the need for practical hustle. Meet with a mentor or trusted friend to make this "diagnosis" of your own situation.

TREP then prescribes a series of targeted next steps to "cure" these gaps, helping you become smarter about the CRE landscape. This includes educational actions to deepen your understanding of industry trends, such as researching office market dynamics or subscribing to key newsletters; skill-building exercises like practicing negotiation tactics or tactical listening; and strategic moves to position yourself for employment, from updating your LinkedIn profile and attending networking events to applying for internships at brokerage firms.

Presented in a simple, editable worksheet format with columns for Item, Notes, Due Date, and Complete, the Prescription encourages accountability and progress tracking. You can check off completed items, add notes on learnings or challenges, and adjust as needed, turning abstract ambitions into a tangible timeline. Typically spanning 9-15 tasks over a few weeks or months, it's flexible enough to tailor to your pace, whether you're a recent graduate hustling part-time or someone balancing a full-time job.

The ultimate purpose is to foster delayed gratification through consistent execution: by following TREP, you'll build a robust network, gain real-world exposure, and demonstrate the initiative that CRE leaders value, ultimately increasing your chances of landing a role at a top firm.

Think of it as your personalized accelerator. Not a magic pill, but a proven regimen to diagnose, educate, and activate your path to becoming a successful tenant rep broker in today's evolving market.

The Prescription Worksheet

PRESCRIPTION FOR SUCCESS IN
COMMERCIAL REAL ESTATE BROKERAGE

ITEM	NOTES	DUE DATE	COMPLETE
01			◯
02			◯
03			◯
04			◯
05			◯
06			◯
07			◯
08			◯
09			◯
10			◯
11			◯

Signature: _Ken Ashley_

Prescription Examples

Example 1: Alex's Real Estate Prescription (Focus: Getting Started as a Tenant Rep Broker)

Item	Notes	DueDate	Complete
1. Research and understand the role of a tenant representative in commercial real estate, including key skills like negotiation and space planning.	Read articles or watch videos on tenant rep basics; note down 5 key skills.	October 10	
2. Secure a part-time job or internship at a brokerage firm to gain initial experience while building your network.	Apply to at least 3 firms. Prepare a resume highlighting any sales or customer service experience.	October 17	
3. Set up a professional social media profiles on LinkedIn and X (Twitter) for networking in CRE.	Follow 50 industry leaders, including Ken Ashley. Post your first update about your interest in real estate.	October 24	
4. Create a "meet sheet" template to track meetings, learnings, and follow-ups.	Use tools like Evernote; practice with a mock meeting.	October 31	
5. Develop a basic tenant rep business plan outlining your goals for the next 6 months.	Include targets for meetings and leads; keep it simple and focused on execution.	November 17	
6. Attend a local CRE networking event or webinar.	Look for free events on Meetup or CREI-related platforms.	November 14	
7. Practice tactical listening by having informational interviews with 2 experienced brokers.	Send follow-up notes with relevant articles based on what you learn.	November 21	
8. Schedule your first 15-minute prospecting calls with potential clients.	Aim for 5 calls; use scripts focused on value rather than sales.	November 28	

Item	Notes	DueDate	Complete
9. Review progress and adjust your business plan based on initial feedback.	Track what's working in your meet sheet.	December 5	
10.			
11.			
12.			
13.			
14.			

Example 2: Jordan's Real Estate Prescription (Focus: Building Networks and Brand in CRE)

Item	Notes	Due Date	Complete
1. Join the CREi community or a similar online group for young brokers to start collaborating.	Attend X Spaces as offered.	October 10	
2. Build your personal brand by posting weekly content on social media about CRE trends.	Start with insights from office market returns in 2025-2026. Aim for engagement.	October 17	
3. Identify 10 potential mentors in tenant representation and reach out for coffee chats.	Use LinkedIn; reference Ken Ashley's advice on delayed gratification in brokerage.	October 24	
4. Implement time management techniques, like scheduling 15-minute meetings only.	Block your calendar; use email drafts for quick follow-ups.	October 31	
5. Attend the CREi Summit or a virtual equivalent to learn from industry leaders.	Budget for it if needed. Focus on relationship-building sessions.	November 7	.

Item	Notes	Due Date	Complete
6. Practice follow-up strategies by sending personalized articles to 5 new contacts.	Use tactical listening from conversations to choose relevant topics.	November 14	
7. Track your networking efforts in a dedicated meet sheet, reviewing weekly.	Note outcomes and plan multiple touchpoints per contact.	November 21	
8. Explore opportunities in the office market, researching companies returning to workspaces.	Compile a list of 10 prospects for tenant rep services.	November 28	
9. Evaluate your brand growth by measuring social media interactions and connections.	Adjust content strategy based on what gets responses.	December 5	
10.			
11.			
12.			
13.			
14.			
15.			

Example 3: Taylor's Real Estate Prescription (Focus: Execution and Hustle in Tenant Rep)

Item	Notes	Due Date	Complete
1. Commit to tenant representation as your entry point, listing pros and cons for motivation.	Remember, it requires skills, such as being a psychologist and negotiator. Prepare for the initial hustle.	October 10	
2. Create a second income stream if needed to support your brokerage startup phase.	Explore flexible gigs. Aim to dedicate 20 hours per week to CRE.	October 17	

3. Develop hustle habits by setting daily prospecting goals, like 10 outreach messages.	Focus on execution over perfection in your business plan.	October 24	
4. Use Evernote or similar for organizing notes from meetings and research.	Digitalize your meet sheet for easy access and updates.	October 31	
5. Conduct three practice negotiations or role-plays with peers.	Simulate tenant rep scenarios to build confidence.	November 7	
6. Follow up with all contacts at least 3 times using learned interests from tactical listening.	Send value-added content, like market reports on office adjustments.	November 14	
7. Join a brokerage that supports young tenant reps and shadow a senior broker.	Research firms like Cushman & Wakefield. Ask about mentorship programs.	November 21	
8. Monitor industry trends, especially office space opportunities in 2025.	Subscribe to CRE newsletters. Note how they apply to your prospects.	November 28	
9. Reflect on your progress, celebrating small wins like new connections.	Update your prescription with new tasks based on learnings.	December 5	
10.			
11.			
12.			
13.			
14.			
15.			

Sales Plan Templates

Sales Plan Example

Area of Focus: _________________

Type of Commercial Real Estate Brokerage Services (Office, Industrial, etc.)

Target Executive (Avatar)

Name: John Smith

Position: CEO of mid-sized manufacturing firm

Age: 45-55

Location: San Francisco Bay Area

Company Size: 100-500 employees

Understand the Executive's Worries and Needs

1. **Worries:**
   - Rising operational costs
   - Inefficient use of existing real estate assets
   - Market volatility and its impact on property values

2. **Needs:**
   - Cost-effective real estate solutions
   - Expert advice on optimizing current properties
   - Strategies for future growth and expansion

Capabilities to Solve the Executive's Problems

- **Brokerage Team Strengths**:
  - Extensive market knowledge and analysis
  - Proven track record of cost-saving strategies
  - Strong negotiation skills to secure favorable terms
  - Comprehensive understanding of property optimization
  - Network of industry contacts and resources

Tactics to Reach Out

1. **Cold Calls**:
   - Aim to make 20 targeted calls per week
   - Use a script focused on understanding the executive's current challenges

2. **Social Media LinkedIn Outreach**:
   - Connect with executives and share relevant industry insights
   - Post weekly articles and updates on market trends

3. **Email Campaigns**:
   - Send personalized emails highlighting specific solutions
   - Follow up with case studies and success stories

4. **Networking Events**:
   - Attend industry conferences and local business events
   - Engage in meaningful conversations and exchange business cards

Goals for Tactics

- **Calls**: 30 calls per week, aiming for a 10% response rate
- **LinkedIn**: 5 new connections per week, 1 post per week

- **Emails**: 20 emails per week, aiming for a 15% open rate
- **Events**: Attend 1 event per month, aiming to secure 5 new contacts per event

Recording Activity

- **Spreadsheet**:
  - Columns: Date, Contact Name, Company, Position, Method of Contact, Response, Follow-Up Date
  - Update daily to ensure accurate tracking of interactions and outcomes

Accountability Function

- **Weekly Reporting**:
  - Submit a report to the senior broker every Friday by 3 PM
  - Include metrics on calls made, emails sent, LinkedIn activity, and events attended
  - Highlight successes and areas for improvement

Campaign Duration

- **Length**: 6 months
- **Review**: Quarterly assessments to evaluate progress and adjust tactics as necessary

Success Metrics

- **Contact Goals**:
  - 50 contacts per week, totaling 1,300 over 6 months
  - Target a 3% success rate to secure 39 meetings
  - Aim to convert 10% of meetings into transactions, resulting in approximately 4 deals

Further Resources

As you embark on your journey as an aspiring commercial real estate (CRE) broker, particularly in tenant representation, these resources will help you build knowledge, establish networks, and develop essential skills. I've expanded the lists with additional recommendations based on current trends, focusing on practical tools for job hunting, staying informed, and connecting with peers. Where relevant, I've included brief descriptions for communities to highlight their value.

Job Search Platforms

These sites are essential for finding entry-level positions, internships, or roles at brokerage firms. Focus on searching for "tenant rep broker" or "commercial real estate analyst" keywords, and don't forget to tailor your resume to emphasize any sales, negotiation, or customer service experience.

- **Handshake**: Ideal for recent graduates and students, connecting you with university-affiliated job postings in CRE.
- **Indeed**: A broad job aggregator with filters for CRE roles; set up alerts for new listings in your area.
- **LinkedIn**: The go-to for professional networking—join CRE groups, follow firms like CBRE or JLL, and use the jobs tab to apply directly.
- **SelectLeaders**: A specialized CRE job network featuring postings from top firms; great for brokerage and investment roles.

- **A.CRE Jobs**: Focused on commercial real estate careers, including analyst and broker positions; powered by Adventures in CRE for targeted opportunities.
- **Bullpen**: Connects freelancers and full-time talent in CRE; useful for project-based gigs to build experience while job hunting.
- Company websites (e.g., Cushman & Wakefield, Colliers, JLL): Many brokerages post openings directly on their careers pages—check regularly for unadvertised roles.

Podcasts

Podcasts are a great way to learn on the go about market trends, negotiation tactics, and industry stories. Start with episodes on tenant rep strategies or office market shifts. You can find a full list of all recommended podcasts at CREiSummit.com. Here's a curated list including timeless favorites and top recommendations:

- **The Weekly Take**: Covers CRE news and insights with a focus on weekly market updates.
- **America's Commercial Real Estate Show**: Hosted by Michael Bull, featuring economists, analysts, and leaders discussing CRE topics like leasing and investment.
- **No Cap by CRE Daily**: Straight-talk discussions on CRE trends, hosted by the CRE Daily team.
- **Powers**: In-depth interviews with CRE leaders, emphasizing hustle and long-term strategies.
- **The TreppWire Podcast**: Focuses on CRE finance, data, and market analysis.
- **The Walker Webcast**: High-profile guests discussing CRE and broader economic impacts.

- **Commercial Investment Real Estate**: From CCIM, covering investment strategies and case studies.

- **The Propcast**: Explores proptech innovations intersecting with CRE.

- **Best Real Estate Investing Advice Ever**: Daily tips from experts, with a CRE angle.

- **The Concrete Voice**: Practical advice for CRE professionals on deals and operations.

Email Subscriptions to Join

Stay ahead of CRE trends with daily or weekly digests on news, analysis, and prep materials. These will help you reference current events in networking conversations or interviews.

- **CRE Daily**: Curated CRE news, trends, and insights delivered daily.

- **CoStar News**: In-depth coverage of CRE transactions, market data, and industry shifts.

- **Morning Brew**: General business news with CRE-relevant sections; great for broader context.

- **Wall Street Prep**: Financial modeling and prep courses via email, useful for CRE analysis skills.

- **Bisnow**: Event-driven CRE news with local and national editions.

- **Commercial Observer**: Focuses on finance, deals, and policy in CRE.

- **Propmodo**: Explores the future of real estate, including tech and sustainability.

- **The Real Deal**: National and regional CRE news, with a focus on major markets.

- **WMRE (Wealth Management Real Estate)**: Insights on CRE investment strategies.
- **REBusinessOnline**: Daily updates on CRE development and leasing news.

Real Estate Communities to Join

Joining communities accelerates networking—attend events, participate in forums, and seek mentorship. Many offer young professional programs tailored to aspiring brokers.

- **CREi (CREi Summit Community)**: An inclusive conference and network for everyone in CRE, the use of digital tools to drive better business development; ideal for young brokers to build connections through annual summits and online groups. Go to www.creisummit.com and sign up for the newsletter.
- **CCIM (Certified Commercial Investment Member) Institute**: A global standard for CRE professionals with advanced coursework in financial and market analysis; benefits include tools, expert access, and a network that boosts transaction volume by 42% on average for designees.
- **SIOR (Society of Industrial and Office Realtors)**: Represents top industrial and office brokers, providing prestige, trust, and deal-making opportunities; members complete over 80,000 deals annually, with programs for career advancement and industry partnerships.
- **CoreNet Global**: A non-profit for corporate real estate pros with nearly 10,000 members worldwide; offers professional development, research, conferences, and chapter-based networking to manage global portfolios.
- **NAIOP (Commercial Real Estate Development Association)**: Leading group for developers and owners, with education,

advocacy, and events; great for learning about development trends and policy.

- **Urban Land Institute (ULI)**: A nonprofit focused on responsible land use and sustainable communities; provides research, forums, and mentorship for emerging CRE leaders.

- **ICSC (International Council of Shopping Centers)**: Global network for retail real estate; offers deal-making events and resources for brokers in shopping centers and mixed-use.

- **CREW (Commercial Real Estate Women) Network**: Empowers women in CRE through leadership development, networking, and advocacy; includes mentorship for young professionals.

Sales & Commercial Real Estate Reading List

Foundational & Timeless

- **How to Win Friends and Influence People – Dale Carnegie**
  A must-read for mastering interpersonal skills. Still relevant 90 years later.

- **The Psychology of Selling – Brian Tracy**
  Classic techniques with an emphasis on mindset and motivation.

- **Think and Grow Rich – Napoleon Hill**
  Not purely sales-focused, but a blueprint for success that significantly influenced sales culture.

Tactical & Practical

- **SPIN Selling – Neil Rackham**
  A research-backed method for complex, consultative sales. Especially useful in B2B.

- **To Sell Is Human – Daniel H. Pink**
  Redefines selling: attune, buoy, and clarify. Highly effective for modern sales professionals navigating persuasion in everyday interactions.

- **Sell with a Story – Paul Smith**
  A guide to using storytelling as a powerful persuasion tool.

Modern & Cutting-Edge

- **Fanatical Prospecting – Jeb Blount**
  No fluff, just hard-hitting, actionable prospecting strategies.
- **Gap Selling – Keenan**
  Teaches how to identify and sell to the "gap" between where the prospect is and where they want to be.
- **Sell or Be Sold – Grant Cardone**
  High-energy, aggressive mindset. Love him or hate him, he motivates.

Mindset & Habits

- **Atomic Habits – James Clear**
  Not a sales book per se, but critical for building consistent success routines.
- **The Slight Edge – Jeff Olson**
  Shows how small daily disciplines create long-term sales success.
- **The Go-Giver – Bob Burg & John David Mann**
  A parable reframing success around value and generosity.

If you're just starting out, begin with *How to Win Friends and Influence People* and *Fanatical Prospecting*. If you're seasoned and want to level up strategy, *The Challenger Sale* and *Gap Selling* are sharp picks.

Commercial Real Estate (CRE) Brokerage Focus

Core CRE Brokerage Sales & Strategy

- **Brokers Who Dominate – Rod Santomassimo**
  Real-life case studies of top-producing CRE brokers and what sets them apart.

- **Knowing Isn't Doing – Rod Santomassimo**
  A follow-up to *Brokers Who Dominate*, focused on executing the right habits and systems.

- **Dominators of Commercial Real Estate Brokerage – Rod Santomassimo**
  Explores the strategies, habits, and mindsets of brokers who consistently outperform peers.

- **Thrive: Ten Prescriptions for Exceptional Performance as a Commercial Real Estate Agent – Blaine Strickland**
  Actionable strategies for business development, time management, and client relationships.

- **Adapt: Disruption Is Coming to Commercial Real Estate Brokerage. Are You Ready? – Blaine Strickland**
  Examines nine disruptive forces transforming the CRE industry and provides strategies to navigate them.

- **Selling Building – Bob Knakal & Rod Santomassimo**
  A strategy-packed and practical framework for brokerage mastery, investor insights, deal-making, and market expertise—particularly NYC-focused.

- **The Millionaire Real Estate Agent – Gary Keller**
  Written for residential agents, but its lead-generation and scaling frameworks apply to CRE as well.

- **SHIFT Commercial – Buddy Norman**
  Helps brokers navigate down markets and find opportunities when others panic.

- **Confessions of a Real Estate Entrepreneur – James A. Randel**
  Teaches brokers how to transition from selling deals to owning them. A crucial mindset shift for long-term wealth building.

Sales Techniques That Translate to CRE

- **Pitch Anything – Oren Klaff**

  Learn how to control the room and structure your narrative using "neuroeconomics" and frame control, especially useful in high-stakes listing pitches.

- **Storyworthy – Matthew Dicks**

  Exceptionally valuable for communicators and salespeople; teaches how to craft compelling, authentic stories to engage prospects and inspire action.

- **Fanatical Prospecting – Jeb Blount**

  Still one of the best books on outbound hustle, cold calling, and appointment setting; table stakes for CRE brokers.

Negotiation, Wealth-Building & Mindset

- **Never Split the Difference – Chris Voss**

  FBI hostage negotiation tactics made practical. Essential for high-dollar lease or investment negotiations.

- **The Real Estate Game – William Poorvu (Harvard Business School)**

  Helps brokers understand deals the way investors do. Critical for investment sales and advisory work.

- **The Personal MBA – Josh Kaufman**

  Sharpens business acumen and broadens perspective. Reminds CRE brokers that they aren't just selling space, but advising on business decisions.

Extra: CRE-Specific Training Resources

- **Massimo Group – Rod Santomassimo**
  One of North America's premier CRE coaching and consulting organizations, offering tailored processes, books, and training for brokers.

- **Barbi Reuter's *CRE Woman's Playbook* (LinkedIn)**
  Not yet a book, but full of practical insights for brokerage success.

- **One More Deal – Blaine Strickland**
  A CRE coaching and training firm that helps brokers grow their business, close more deals, and transition from agent to owner through personalized coaching and strategic workshops.

Resources: Links and Websites

300 Months https://www.kenashleycre.com/blog/300-months

IBIS World Market Research. Market size and recent performance (2015-2030). https://www.ibisworld.com/united-states/industry/commercial-real-estate/2009/

Hustle as a Strategy https://www.kenashleycre.com/blog/hustle-as-a-strategy

My First Cold Call https://www.kenashleycre.com/blog/my-first-cold-call?rq=cold

Commercial Real Estate Influencers/Innovators https://www.creisummit.com/crei-list/

Sale Plan Templates https://templatelab.com/sales-plan-templates/

CREi Summit https://www.creisummit.com